ESTATE PUBLICATIONS

GLOUCES...RE

G000113850

Street maps with index
Administrative Districts
Population Gazetteer
Road Map with index
Postcodes

COUNTY RED BOOKS

This atlas is intended for those requiring street maps of the historical and commercial centres of towns within the county. Each locality is normally presented on one or two pages and although, with many small towns, this space is sufficient to portray the whole urban area, the maps of large towns and cities are for centres only and are not intended to be comprehensive. Such coverage in Super and Local Red Books (see page 2).

Every effort has been made to verify the accuracy of information in this book but the publishers cannot accept responsibility for expense or loss caused by any error or omission. Information that will be of assistance to the user of these maps will be welcomed.

The representation of a road, track or footpath on the maps in this atlas is no evidence of the existence of a right of way.

Street plans prepared and published by ESTATE PUBLICATIONS, Bridewell House, TENTERDEN, KENT. The Publishers acknowledge the co-operation of the local authorities of towns represented in this atlas.

Ordnance Survey® This product includes mapping data licensed from Ordnance Survey® with the permission of the Controller of Her Majesty's Stationery Office.

COUNTY RED BOOK

GLOUCESTERSHIRE

contains street maps for each town centre

SUPER & LOCAL RED BOOKS

are street atlases with comprehensive local coverage

GLOUCESTER & CHELTENHAM

including: Bishops Cleeve, Brockworth, Hardwicke, Quedgeley, Shurdington, Upton St. Leonards etc.

STROUD & NAILSWORTH

including: Cam, Dursley, Minchinhampton, Painswick, Stonehouse, Tetbury etc.

CONTENTS

COUNTY ADMINISTRATIVE DISTRICTS: pages 4-5

GAZETTEER INDEX TO ROAD MAP: pages 6-7
(with populations)

COUNTY ROAD MAP: pages 8-11

TOWN CENTRE STREET MAPS:

LEGEND TO STREET MAPS

One-Way Street	→	Post Office	●
Pedestrianized	▨	Public Convenience	C
Car Park	P	Place of Worship	+

Scale of street plans: 4 Inches to 1 mile (unless otherwise stated on the map).

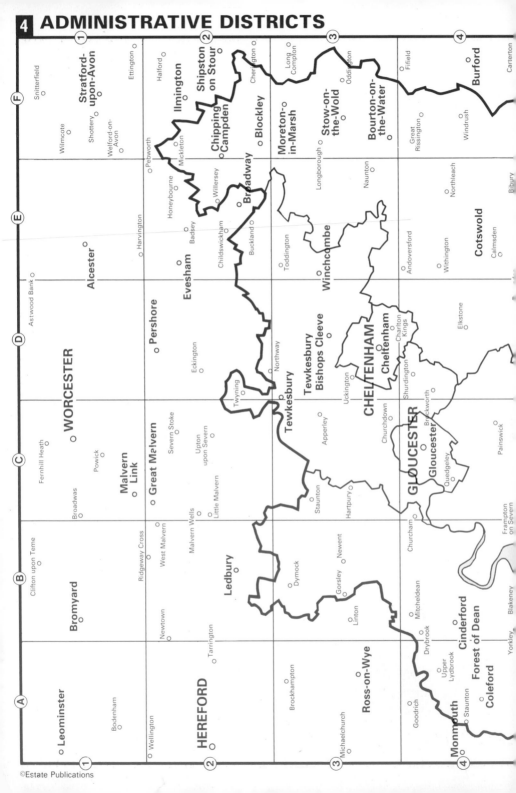

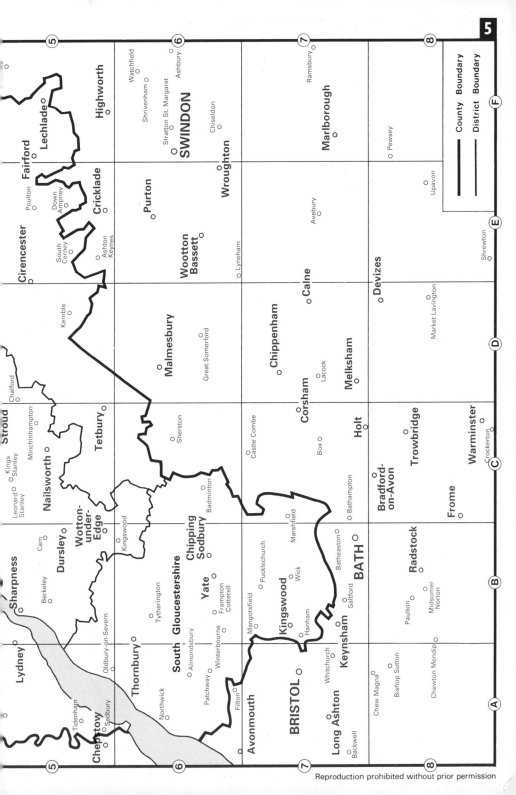

5

County Boundary

District Boundary

Watchfield

Ashbury

Highworth

Shrivenham

Stratton St. Margaret

Lechlade

Fairford

Chiseldon

Ramsbury

SWINDON

Poulton

Down Ampney

Cricklade

Purton

Wroughton

Marlborough

Pewsey

Cirencester

South Cerney

Ashton Keynes

Wootton Bassett

Avebury

Upavon

Kemble

Lyneham

Calne

Devizes

Shrewton

Chalford

Malmesbury

Great Somerford

Chippenham

Market Lavington

Stroud

Minchinhampton

Sherston

Lacock

Melksham

Kings Stanley

Nailsworth

Tetbury

Castle Combe

Corsham

Box

Holt

Trowbridge

Warminster

Leonard Stanley

Wotton-under-Edge

Kingswood

Badminton

Bradford-on-Avon

Crockerton

Dursley

Cam

Berkeley

Chipping Sodbury

Marshfield

Bathampton

Frome

Sharpness

Tytherington

Yate

Frampton Cotterell

Pucklechurch

Wick

Batheaston

BATH

Radstock

Lydney

Dursley

South Gloucestershire

Almondsbury

Winterbourne

Mangotsfield

Kingswood

Hanham

Saltford

Paulton

Midsomer Norton

Thornbury

Patchway

Hanham

Keynsham

Tidenham

Sedbury

Northwick

Filton

Avonmouth

Whitchurch

Chewton Mendip

Chepstow

BRISTOL

Long Ashton

Chew Magna

Bishop Sutton

Backwell

GAZETTEER INDEX TO ROAD MAP
with Populations

County of Gloucestershire population **748,734**

Districts:
Cheltenham **103,115**
Cotswold **73,965**
Forest of Dean **75,351**
Gloucester **101,608**
Kingswood **89,717**
Northavon **130,647**
Stroud **103,622**
Tewkesbury **70,709**

Ablington		11 H5
Acton Turville		9 E8
Adlestrop		10 K3
Alderley **72**		9 D7
Alderton **681**		10 G2
Aldsworth **233**		11 J5
Alkington **641**		*
Almondsbury **7,317**		9 B8
Alstone		10 G3
Alveston **3,060**		9 C7
Alvington **457**		9 B6
Amberley		11 E6
Ampney Crucis **561**		11 H6
Ampney St Mary **119**		11 H6
Ampney St. Peter **107**		11 H6
Andoversford **547**		10 G4
Apperley		10 E3
Arlingham **377**		8 D5
Arlington		11 H5
Ashchurch **5,999**		10 F3
Ashleworth **476**		8 E3
Ashley **107**		11 F7
Ashton Keynes		11 H7
Aston Magna		10 J2
Aston Subedge **80**		10 J2
Aust **450**		9 B7
Avening **1,038**		11 E6
Awkley		9 B8
Awre **1,614**		8 C5
Aylburton **372**		9 B6
Badgeworth **1,168**		10 F4
Badminton **248**		9 E8
Bagendon **240**		11 G5
Barnsley **142**		11 H6
Barnwood		10 E4
Barrington **201**		11 J5
Barton		10 H3
Batsford **142**		10 J2
Baughspring		9 B6
Baunton **266**		11 G6
Beachley		9 B7
Bentham		10 F4
Berkeley **1,550**		9 C6
Berry Hill		8 B5
Beverston **134**		11 E7
Bevington		9 C6
Bibury **570**		11 H5
Birdlip		11 F5
Birdwood		8 D4
Bishop's Cleeve **7,186**		10 F3
Bisley-with-Lypiatt **2,118**		11 F5
Bitton **9,033**		9 C9
Blaisdon **253**		8 C4
Blakeney		8 C5
Bledington **424**		10 K4
Blockley **1,668**		10 J2
Boddington **260**		10 F3
Bournes Green		11 F6
Bourton-on-the-Hill **321**		10 J3
Bourton-on-the-Water **2,905**		10 J4
Box		11 E6
Boxbush		8 D5
Boxwell with Leighterton **210**		11 E7
Breadstone		9 C6
Bream **3,556**		9 B6
Bridge Yate		9 C9
Brierley		8 C4
Brimpsfield **266**		11 F5
Broad Campden		10 J2
Broadwell (Stow on the Wold) **351**		10 J3
Broadwell		8 B5

Brockhampton		10 G4
Brockweir		9 B6
Brockworth **6,649**		10 F4
Bromsberrow **182**		*
Brookethorpe-with-Whaddon **300**		11 E5
Buckland **247**		10 H2
Bulley		8 D4
Cainscross (Stroud) **5,879**		*
Calmsden		11 G5
Cam **8,099**		9 D6
Cambridge **1,792**		9 D6
Cerney Wick		11 H7
Chaceley **120**		10 E3
Chalford **4,677**		11 E6
Charfield **2,231**		9 D7
Charingworth		10 J2
Charlton Abbots		10 G3
Charlton Kings **7,923**		10 G4
Chedworth **763**		11 H5
Cheltenham **86,996**		10 F4
Cherington **119**		11 F6
Chipping Campden **1,997**		10 J2
Chipping Sodbury **4,596**		9 D8
Christchurch		8 B5
Churcham **630**		8 D4
Churchdown **10,319**		10 F4
Cinderford **7,653**		8 C4
Cirencester **17,085**		11 G6
Clapton-on-the-Hill **94**		10 J4
Clearwell		8 B5
Cleeve Hill **3,672**		10 G3
Clifford's Mesne		8 C4
Coaley **779**		9 D6
Coalpit Heath		9 C8
Coalway		8 B5
Coates **463**		11 G6
Coberley **284**		10 F4
Codrington		9 D8
Cold Ashton **239**		9 D9
Cold Aston **214**		10 H4
Coleford **5,069**		8 B5
Colesbourne **119**		11 G5
Coln Rogers		11 H5
Coln St. Aldwyn's **260**		11 J5
Coln St. Dennis **192**		11 H5
Compton Abdale **126**		10 H4
Condicote **137**		10 J3
Coombe Hill **3,145**		10 F3
Corse **534**		*
Cowley **311**		11 F5
Cranham **452**		11 F5
Cromhall **814**		9 C7
Cromhall Common		9 C7
Culkerton		11 F7
Cutsdean **72**		10 H3
Daglingworth **246**		*
Daylesford		10 K3
Deerhurst **887**		10 E3
Didbrook		10 H3
Didmarton **429**		11 E7
Dixton		10 G3
Dodington **8,715**		9 D8
Donnington **74**		10 J3
Doughton		11 E7
Dowdeswell **174**		10 G4
Down Ampney **502**		11 H6
Down Hatherley **433**		10 E4
Doynton **303**		9 D9
Draycott		10 J2
Driffield **146**		11 H6
Drybrook **2,742**		8 C4
Dumbleton **510**		10 G2
Duntisbourne Abbots **227**		11 F5
Duntisbourne Leer		11 G6
Duntisbourne Rouse **81**		11 G5
Dursley **5,687**		9 D6
Dymock **1,283**		8 C3
Dyrham & Hinton **277**		9 D9
Eastcombe		11 F6
Easter Compton		9 B8

Eastington with Northleach **1,462**		11 H5
Eastington (Leonard Stanley) **1,469**		9 D6
Eastleach Martin		11 J6
Eastleach Turville **299**		11 J5
Ebrington **441**		10 J2
Edge		11 E5
Edge End		8 B5
Edgeworth **85**		11 F5
Elberton		9 B7
Elkstone **226**		11 G5
Ellwood		8 B5
Elmore **198**		8 D4
Elmore Back		8 D4
Elmstone Hardwicke **362**		10 F3
Elton		8 C5
Engine Common		9 C8
English Bicknor **414**		8 B4
Epney		8 D5
Evenlode **153**		10 J3
Ewen		11 G6
Fairford **2,919**		11 J6
Falfield **471**		9 C7
Farleys End		8 D4
Farmcote		10 H3
Farmington **100**		10 H4
Fiddington		10 F3
Flaxley		8 C4
Ford		10 H3
Forthampton **169**		10 E3
Fossebridge **1,421**		11 H5
Foxcote		10 G4
Frampton Cotterell **5,989**		9 C8
Frampton Mansell		11 F6
Frampton on Severn **1,383**		8 D5
Fretherne with Saul **640**		8 D5
Frocester **190**		9 D6
Fyfield		11 J6
Ganders Green		8 C4
Gloucester **94,256**		10 E4
Golden Valley		10 F4
Gorsley		8 C3
Gotherington **994**		10 F3
Great Rissington **315**		10 J4
Great Washbourne		10 G2
Great Witcombe **90**		11 F5
Gretton		10 G3
Guiting Power **331**		10 H3
Hailes		10 G3
Hallen		9 B8
Halmore		9 C6
Ham & Stone **704**		9 C6
Hambrook		9 B8
Hamfallow **1,124**		*
Hampen		10 D4
Hampnett **53**		10 H4
Hanham **5,776**		9 C9
Hardwick		10 F3
Hardwicke **3,237**		8 D5
Harescombe **278**		11 E5
Haresfield **349**		11 E5
Harnhill		11 H6
Hartpury **663**		8 D3
Hasfield **136**		10 E3
Hatherop **151**		11 J6
Hawkesbury **1,145**		9 D8
Hawkesbury Upton		9 D8
Hawling **110**		10 H4
Hazleton **158**		10 H4
Hempsted		8 E4
Hewelsfield **410**		9 B6
Highleadon & Rudford **214**		8 D4
Highnam **2,130**		8 D4
Hill **91**		9 C7
Hillesley & Tresham **518**		9 D7
Hinton **1,147**		9 D9
Horsley **767**		11 E6
Horton **362**		9 D8
Hucclecote (Gloucester) **788**		*
Huntley **1,082**		8 D4
Hyde		11 F6

Place	Pop.	Ref.
Icomb	97	10 J4
Ingst		9 B7
Innsworth	1,827	10 E4
Iron Acton	1,322	9 C8
Itchington		9 C8
Kemble	762	11 G6
Kempley	288	8 C3
Kempsford	1,229	11 J6
Kent's Green		8 D4
Kilcot		8 C3
Kineton		10 H3
King's Stanley	2,618	11 E6
Kingscote	328	11 E6
Kingswood (Bristol)	48,117	9 C9
Kingswood (Wotton-u-Edge)	1,232	9 D7
Latteridge		9 C8
Laverton		10 H2
Lechlade	2,293	11 J6
Leckhampton	3,973	10 F4
Leighterton with Boxwell	210	11 E7
Leonard Stanley	1,501	9 E6
Little Badminton		9 E8
Little Barrington		11 J5
Little Rissington	893	10 J4
Little Sodbury		9 D8
Littledean	1,258	8 C5
Littleton upon Severn		9 B7
Long Newnton	179	11 F7
Longborough	507	10 J3
Longford	1,209	10 E4
Longhope	1,491	8 C4
Longney	183	8 D5
Lower Cam		9 D6
Lower Lydbrook		8 B4
Lower Slaughter	215	10 J4
Lower Swell		10 J3
Lydney	7,413	9 B6
Maisemore	487	8 E4
Mangotsfield	5,150	9 C9
Mangotsfield Rural	5,389	*
Marshfield	1,464	9 D9
Matson		10 E4
Maugersbury	150	*
Meysey Hampton	517	11 H6
Mickleton	1,551	10 J1
Milbury Heath		9 C7
Mile End		8 B5
Milkwall		8 B5
Minchinhampton	5,173	11 E6
Minsterworth	440	8 D4
Miserden	429	11 F5
Mitcheldean	2,632	8 C4
Moreton Valence	226	8 D5
Moreton-in-Marsh	2,802	10 J3
Morton		9 C7
Nailsworth	5,242	11 E6
Naunton	309	10 H4
Netherend		9 B6
New Grounds		9 D6
Newent	5,373	8 D3
Newland	923	8 B5
Newnham	1,192	8 C5
Newport		9 C6
Nibley		9 C8
North Cerney	541	11 G5
North Nibley	803	9 D7
Northleach with Eastington	1,462	11 H5
Northway		10 F2
Northwick		9 B8
Northwood Green		8 D4
Norton	407	10 E3
Notgrove	105	10 H4
Nympsfield	326	9 E6
Oakle Street		8 D4
Oakridge		11 F6
Oddington	387	10 K3
Old Sodbury		9 D8
Oldbury on Severn	695	9 B7
Oldbury on the Hill		11 E7
Oldland	13,855	9 C9
Olverston	2,045	9 B7
Over		9 B8
Owlpen	36	*
Oxenhall	223	*
Oxenton	184	10 F3
Ozleworth	31	*
Painswick	3,013	11 E5
Parkend		8 B5
Patchway	11,017	9 B8
Pauntley	158	*
Paxford		10 J2
Pilning & Severn Beach	2,767	9 B8
Pitchcombe	248	11 E5
Plusterwine		9 B6
Poole Keynes	158	11 G7
Poolhill		8 D3
Poulton	354	11 H6
Prescott	90	*
Prestbury	7,403	10 G4
Preston	251	11 G6
Preston		8 C2
Pucklechurch	2,921	9 C9
Purton		9 C6
Quedgeley	7,352	8 D5
Quenington	514	11 J6
Randwick	1,470	11 E5
Rangeworthy	468	9 C8
Redbrook		8 B5
Redmarley D'Abitot	774	8 D3
Redwick		9 B8
Rendcomb	212	11 G5
Rockhampton	176	9 C7
Rodborough (Stroud)	5,367	*
Rodley		8 D5
Rodmarton	247	11 F6
Ruardean	1,435	8 B4
Ruardean Woodside		8 C4
Rudford & Highleadon	214	8 D4
Rudgeway		9 B8
Ruspidge	2,425	8 C5
Ryton		8 D3
St Briavels	1,329	9 B6
Saintbury	76	10 H2
Salperton		10 H4
Sandhurst	458	10 E4
Sapperton	370	11 F6
Saul		8 D5
Sedbury		9 B7
Sevenhampton	376	10 G4
Severn Beach & Pilning	2,767	9 B8
Sezincote	93	10 J3
Sharpness		9 C6
Sheepscombe		11 E5
Shepperdine		9 B7
Sherborne	293	11 J5
Shipton	317	10 G4
Shipton Moyne	293	*
Shorncote		11 G6
Shurdington	2,242	10 F4
Shuthonger		10 E2
Siddington	1,345	11 G6
Siston	2,155	9 C9
Slad		11 E5
Slimbridge	1,113	9 D6
Snowshill	156	10 H2
Somerford Keynes	410	11 G7
Soundwell		9 C9
South Cerney	2,890	11 G6
Southam	760	10 G3
Southrop	223	11 J6
Standish	237	*
Stanton	222	10 H2
Stanway	322	10 H3
Staunton	542	8 D3
Staunton Coleford	267	*
Staverton	680	10 F4
Stinchcombe	410	9 D6
Stoke Gifford	12,342	9 C8
Stoke Orchard	312	10 F3
Stone & Ham	704	9 C7
Stonehouse	6,749	11 E5
Stow-on-the-Wold	1,999	10 J3
Stroat		9 B6
Stroud	11,677	11 E5
Sudeley	92	*
Sudgrove		11 F5
Swell	331	*
Swindon	1,780	10 F3
Syde	32	11 F5
Syreford		10 G4
Tarlton		11 F6
Taynton	403	8 D4
Teddington	420	10 F2
Temple Guiting	367	10 H3
Tetbury	4,618	11 E7
Tetbury Upton	447	11 F7
Tewkesbury	9,488	10 E3
The Camp		11 F5
The Leigh	331	10 E3
The Quarry		9 D6
Thornbury	12,617	9 C7
Througham		11 F5
Thrupp	1,768	11 E6
Tibberton	822	8 D4
Tidenham	4,943	9 B7
Tirley	385	10 E3
Tockington		9 B8
Toddington	418	10 G3
Todenham	221	10 K2
Tormarton	366	9 D8
Tortworth	129	9 C7
Tresham & Hillesley	518	9 D7
Trow Green		8 B5
Tuffley		10 E4
Turkdean	104	10 H4
Twigworth	434	10 E4
Twyning	1,513	10 F2
Tytherington	560	9 C7
Uckington	313	10 F3
Uley	1,121	9 D6
Ullenwood		10 F4
Up Hatherley	2,963	10 F4
Upleadon	231	8 D3
Upper Framilode		8 D5
Upper Lydbrook	2,323	8 B4
Upper Slaughter	204	10 J4
Upper Soudley		8 C5
Upper Swell		10 J3
Upton Cheney		9 C9
Upton St. Leonards	1,674	10 E4
Walton Cardiff	58	*
Wanswell		9 C6
Wapley		9 D8
West Dean	12,139	*
West Littleton		9 D9
Westbury-on-Severn	1,737	8 D4
Westcote	197	10 J4
Westerleigh	3,054	9 C8
Weston sub Edge	389	10 H2
Westonbirt with Lasborough	165	11 E7
Whaddon with Brookthorpe	300	11 E5
Whelford		11 J6
Whitecroft		8 B5
Whiteshill & Ruscombe	1,266	11 E5
Whiteway		11 F5
Whitfield		9 C7
Whitminster	495	8 D5
Whittington	126	10 G4
Wibdon		9 B6
Wick & Abson	1,940	9 C9
Wickwar	1,552	9 D7
Willersey	378	10 H2
Winchcombe	4,835	10 G3
Windrush	109	11 J5
Winson	59	11 H5
Winstone	221	11 F5
Winterbourne	8,811	9 C8
Withington	486	10 G4
Woodchester	1,073	11 E6
Woodcroft		9 B7
Woodford		9 C7
Woodmancote	2,912	10 G3
Woodmancote		11 G5
Woolaston	1,299	9 B6
Wormington		10 G2
Wotton-under-Edge	5,635	9 D7
Wyck Rissington	103	10 E4
Yanworth	124	11 H5
Yate	19,777	9 D8
Yorkley		8 C5

Population figures are based upon the 1991 census and relate to the local authority or parish as constituted at that date. Places with no population figure form part of a larger local authority area or parish. Boundaries of local authority areas are shown on pages 4-5. Population figures in bold type.

*Parish not shown on maps pages 8-11 due to limitation of scale.

7

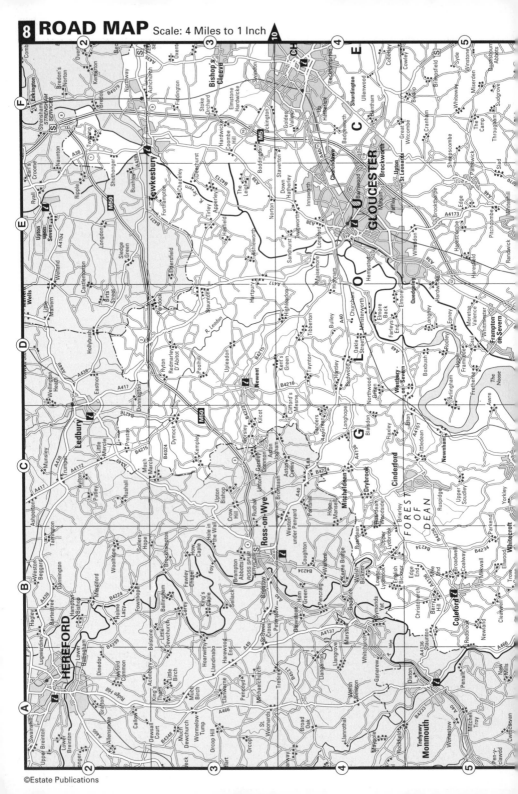

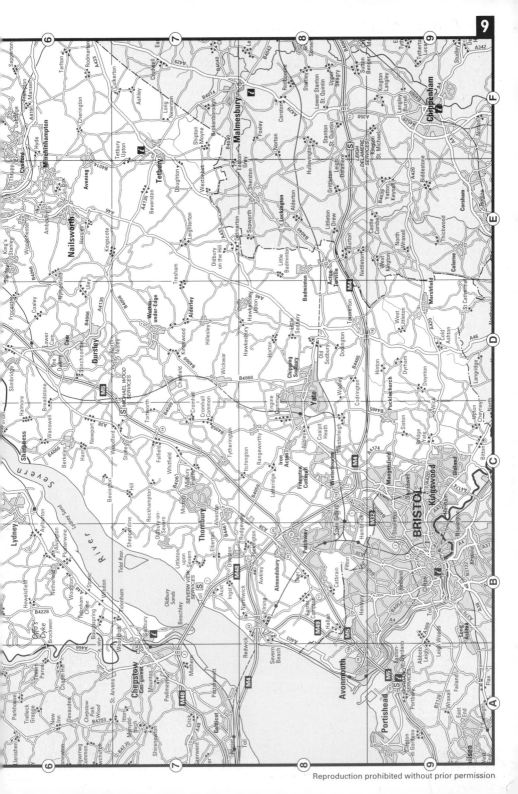

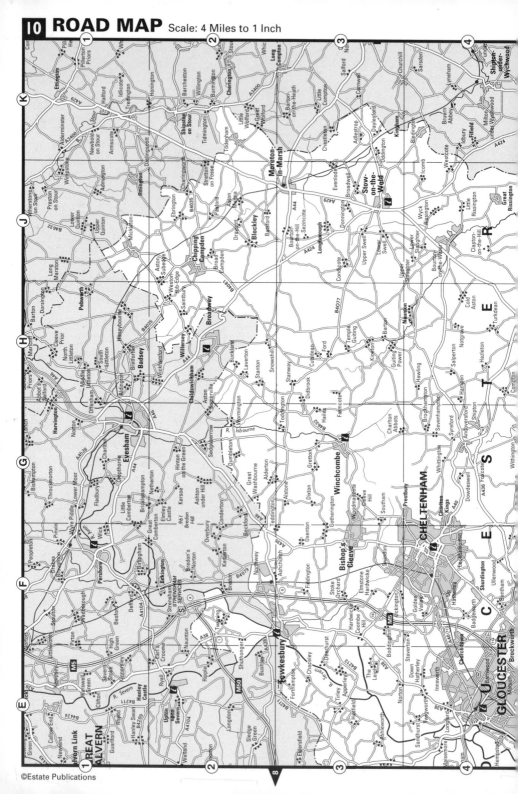

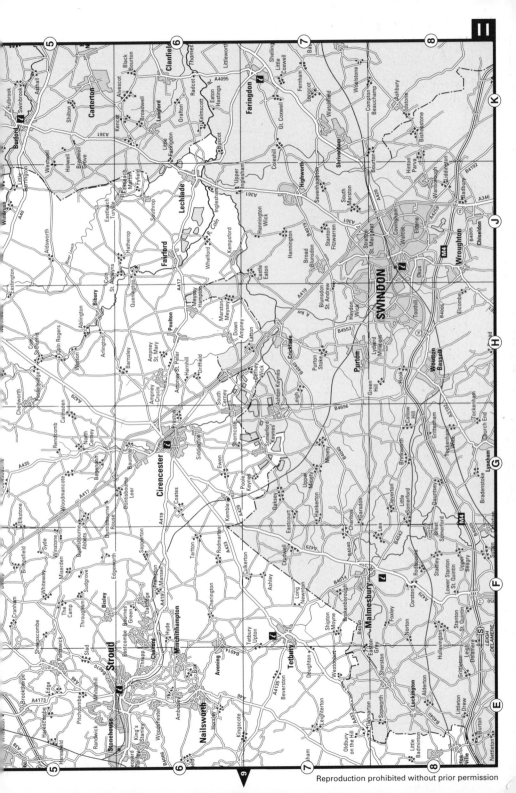

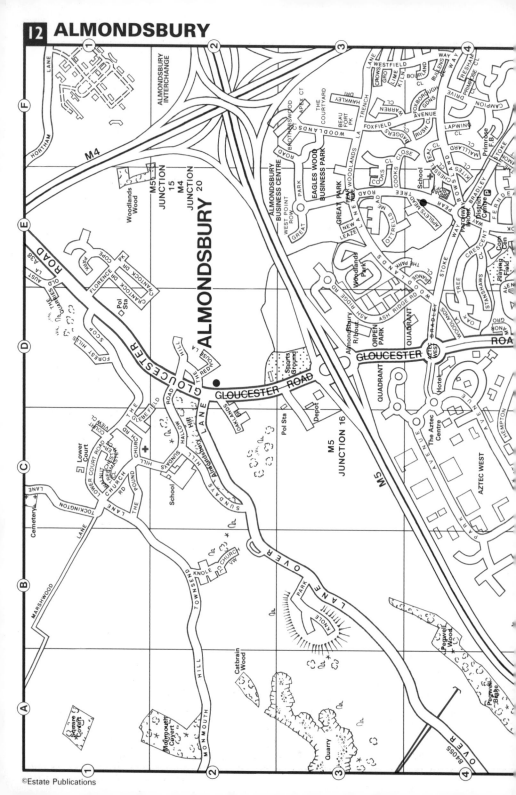

©Estate Publications

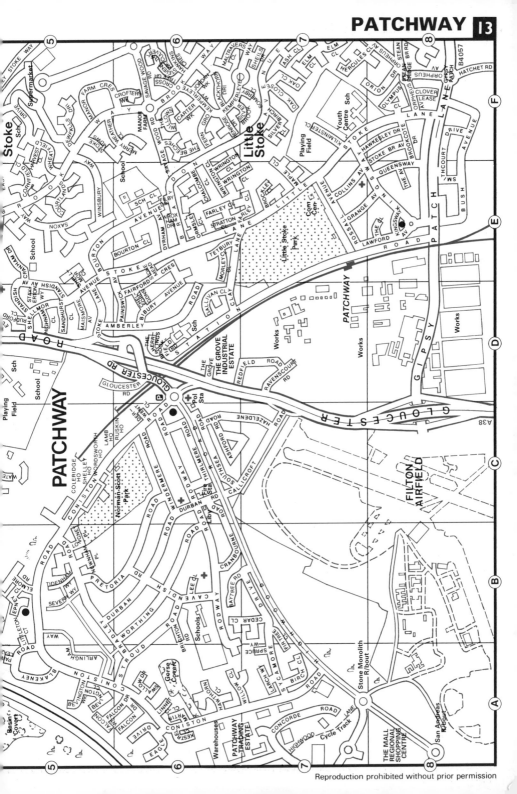

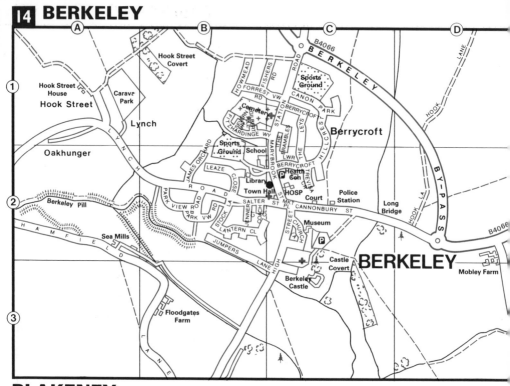

BLAKENEY

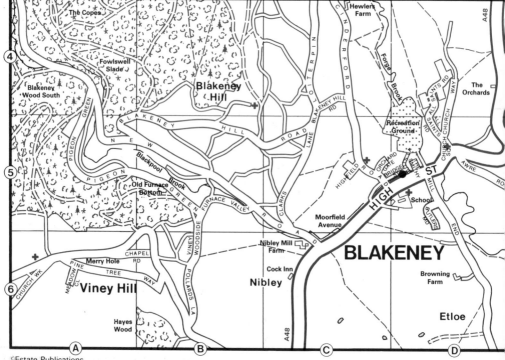

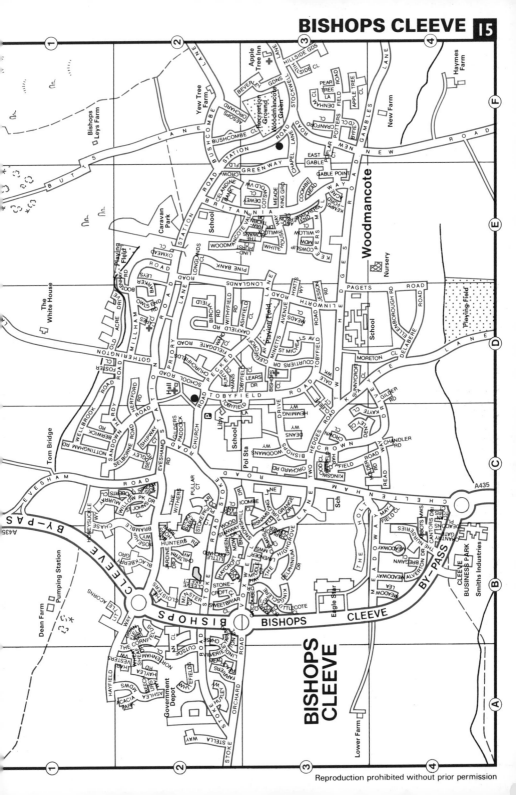

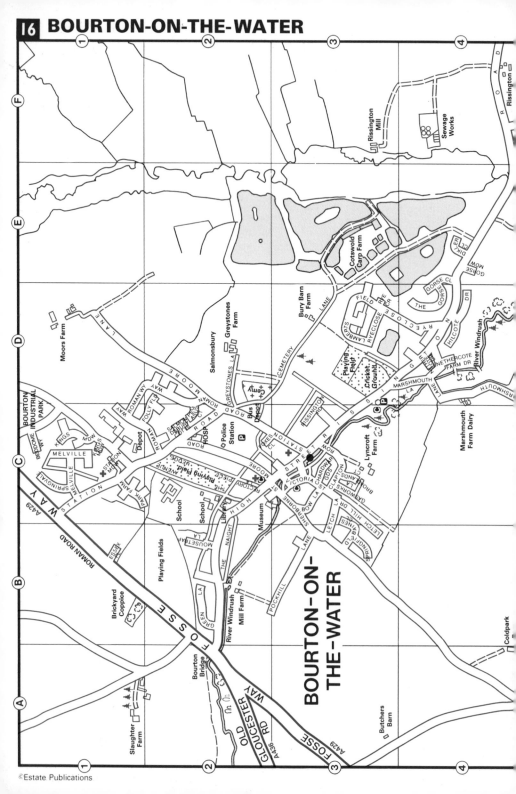

BOURTON-ON-THE-WATER

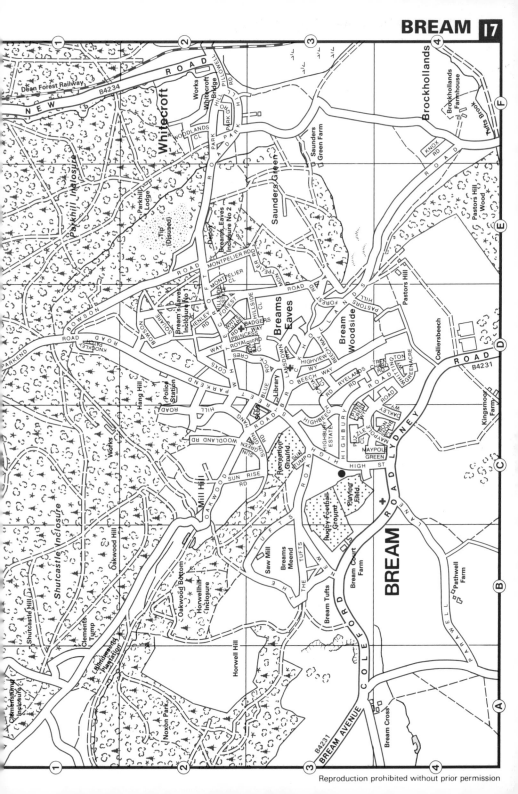

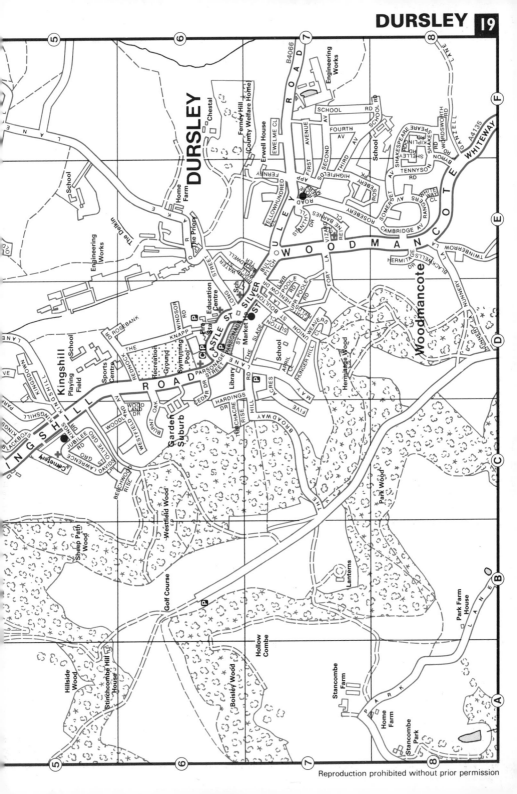

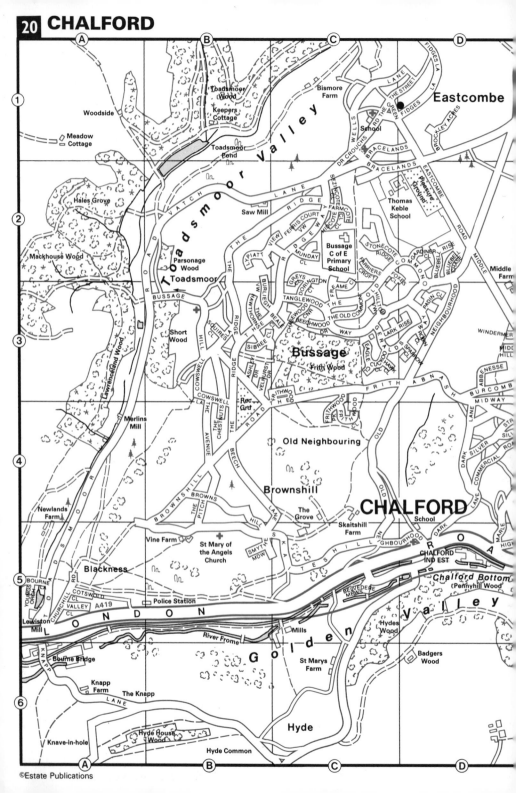

Eastcombe

Toadsmoor Wood
Keepers Cottage
Bismore Farm
Woodside
Meadow Cottage
Toadsmoor Pond
School
Brockley Acres
Bracelands

Hales Grove
Saw Mill
Thomas Keble School
Pleasure Ground

Mackhouse Wood
Parsonage Wood
Toadsmoor
Bussage C of E Primary School
Stonecote
Gardiner
Bluebell Rise
Middle Farm

Short Wood
Farriers Croft
Lark Rise
Windermere

Bussage
Frith Wood
Merlins Mill
Rec Grd
Old Neighbouring

Brownshill
Newlands Farm
The Grove
CHALFORD
School

Vine Farm
St Mary of the Angels Church
Skaitshill Farm
CHALFORD IND EST
Chalford Bottom
(Pennyhill Wood)

Blackness
Police Station
A419
Hydes Wood

Lewiston Mill
Belvedere Mews
Mills
River Frome
St Marys Farm
Badgers Wood

Bourne Bridge
Knapp Farm
The Knapp
Golden Valley
Hyde

Knave-in-hole
Hyde House Wood
Hyde Common

©Estate Publications

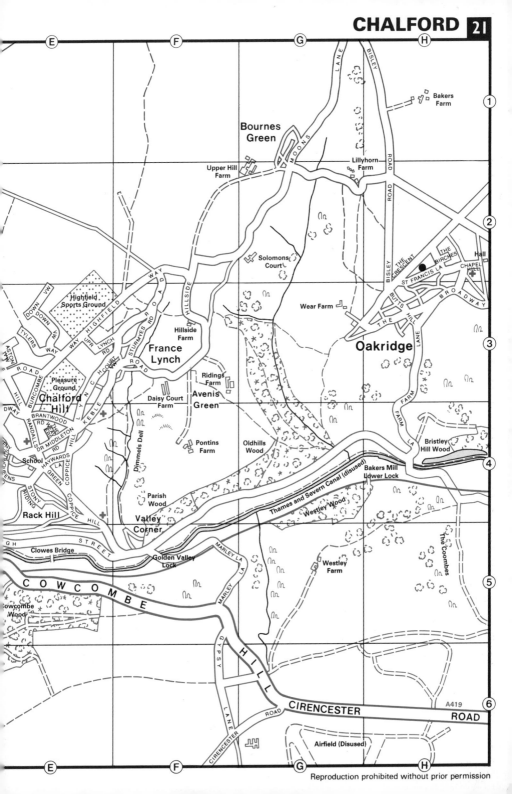

Bakers Farm

Bournes Green

Upper Hill Farm

Lillyhorn Farm

Solomons Court

Hall

CHAPEL HILL

THE BIRCHES

St FRANCIS LA

THE CRESCENT

Highfield Sports Ground

Hillside Farm

Wear Farm

THE BUTTS

Oakridge

BROADWAY

France Lynch

Pleasure Ground

Chalford Hill

Ridings Farm

Avenis Green

Daisy Court Farm

School

Pontins Farm

Oldhills Wood

Bristley Hill Wood

Dimmels Dell

Parish Wood

Bakers Mill Lower Lock

Thames and Severn Canal (disused)

Westley Wood

Rack Hill

Valley Corner

The Coombes

Clowes Bridge

Golden Valley Lock

Westley Farm

COWCOMBE

Cowcombe Wood

HILL

GYPSY LANE

CIRENCESTER ROAD

A419

Airfield (Disused)

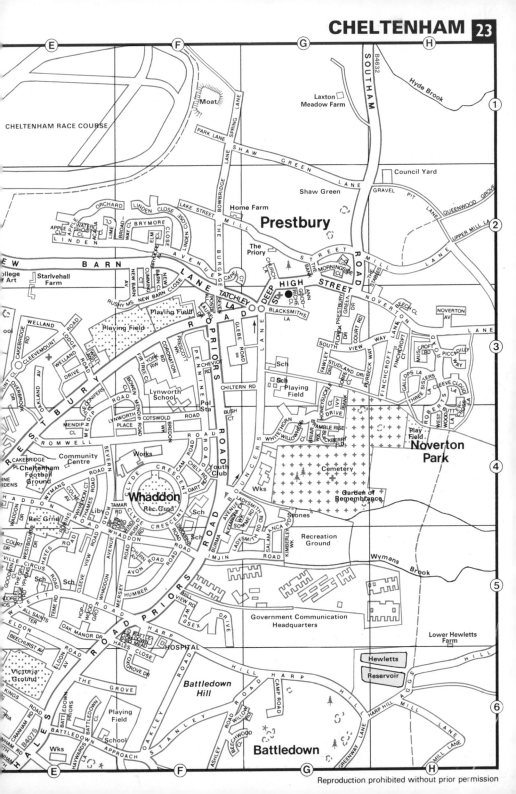

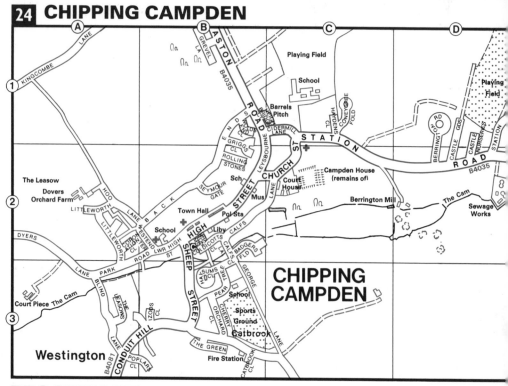

CHIPPING CAMPDEN

BROCKWORTH

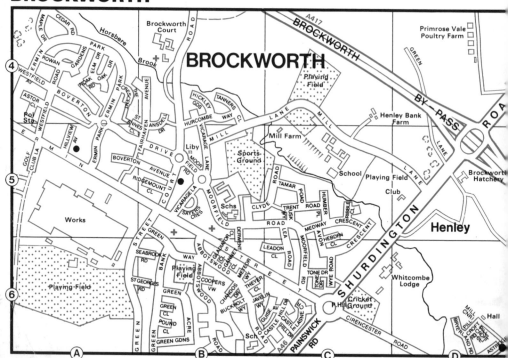

BROCKWORTH

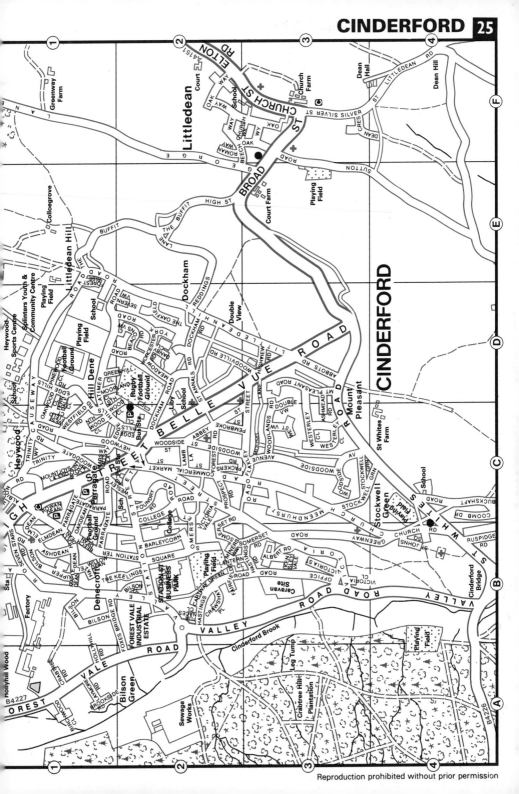

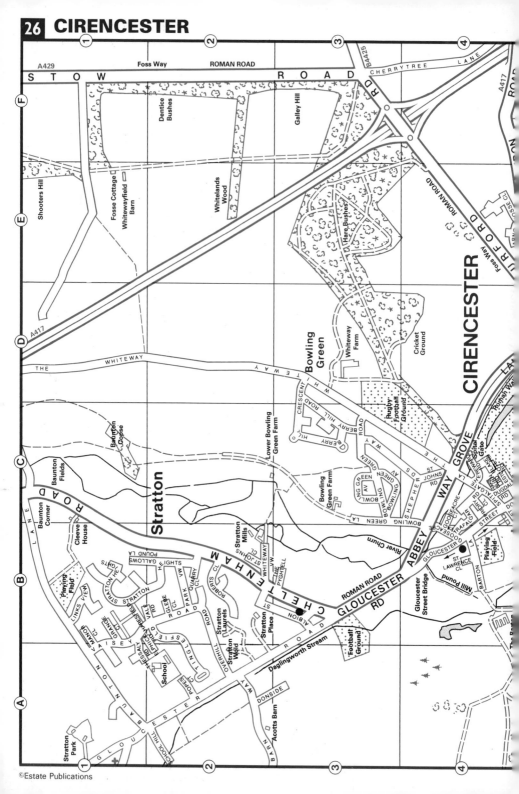

A429
Foss Way   ROMAN ROAD
S T O W   R O A D
A417
B4425
CHERRYTREE   LANE

Dentice Bushes
Galley Hill

Shooters Hill
Fosse Cottage
Whitewayfield Barn
Whitelands Wood

Hare Bushes

ROMAN ROAD

Foss Way

CIRENCESTER

A417

CRICKLADE

Whiteway Farm
Cricket Ground
Bowling Green

Rugby Football Ground
THE WHITEWAY
A417
THE

Baunton Copse

Lower Bowling Green Farm

CRESCENT
BERRY HILL
ROAD
BERRY HILL
WAY
THE

Stratton

Baunton Fields
Baunton Corner

Bowling Green Farm

SHEPHERD'S

ST JOHNS RD

ABBEY   WAY   GROVE   LANE

Bagendon Way
Spital Gate

Cleeve House

ROAD
GALLOWS
POUND LA

Stratton Mills
Stratton Laurels
Stratton Weld
School
Stratton Place

CHELTENHAM

ST JOHNS
WHITEWAY

River Churn

GLOUCESTER   RD
ROMAN ROAD

ALBION ST

GLOUCESTER RD

Playing Field
ST LAWRENCE CL

Mill Pound

Links View
MANOR
Playing Field
Grange
Baisey

School
Ovenhill

Daglingworth Stream

Football Ground

Gloucester Street Bridge

Stratton Park
GLOUCESTER

BAUNTON LANE
SCHOOL HILL

Acotts Barn
DONSIDE
BARN

© Estate Publications

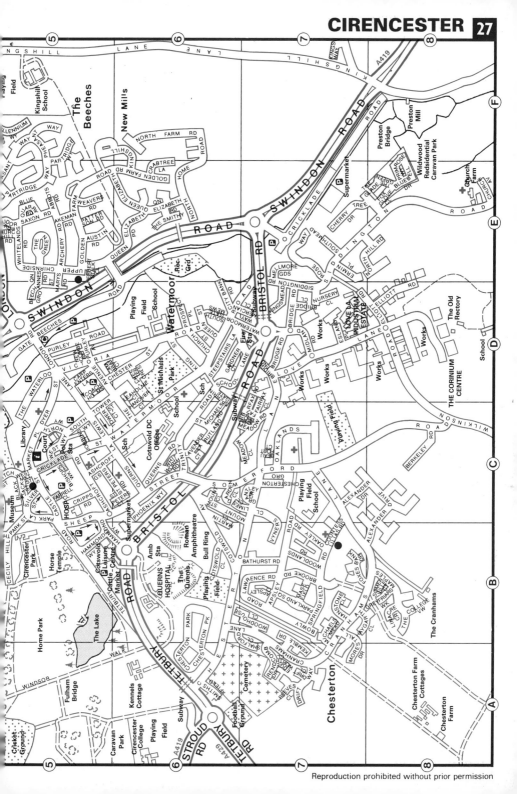

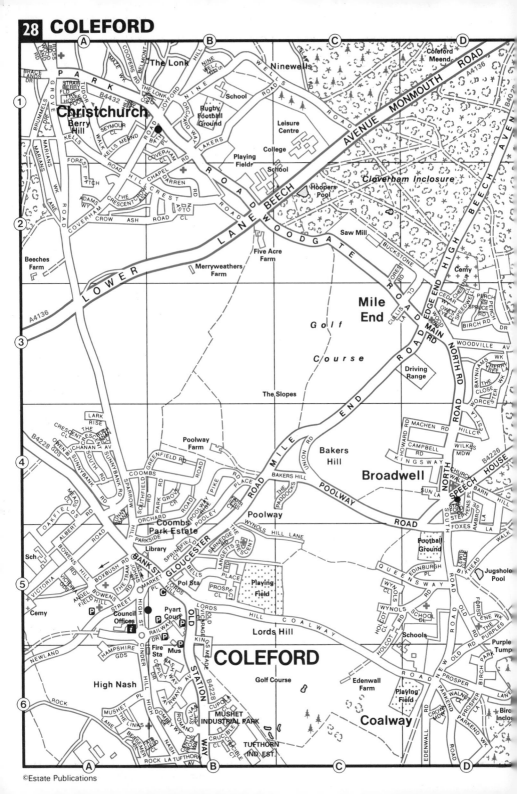

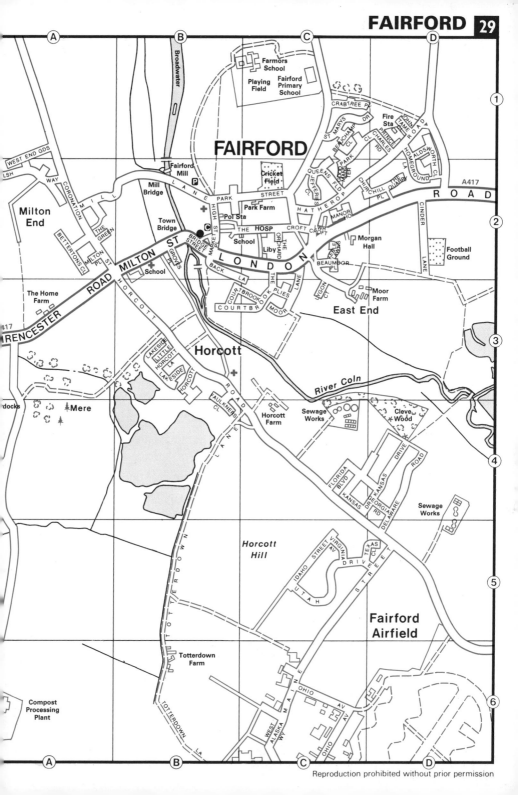

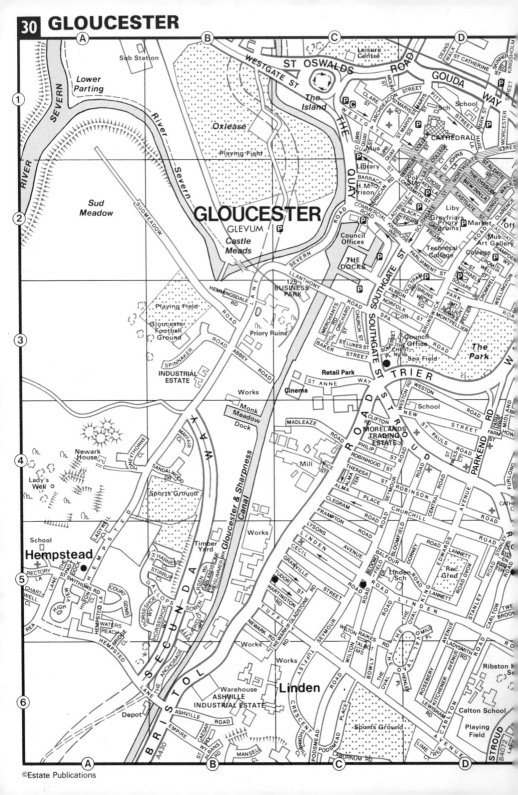

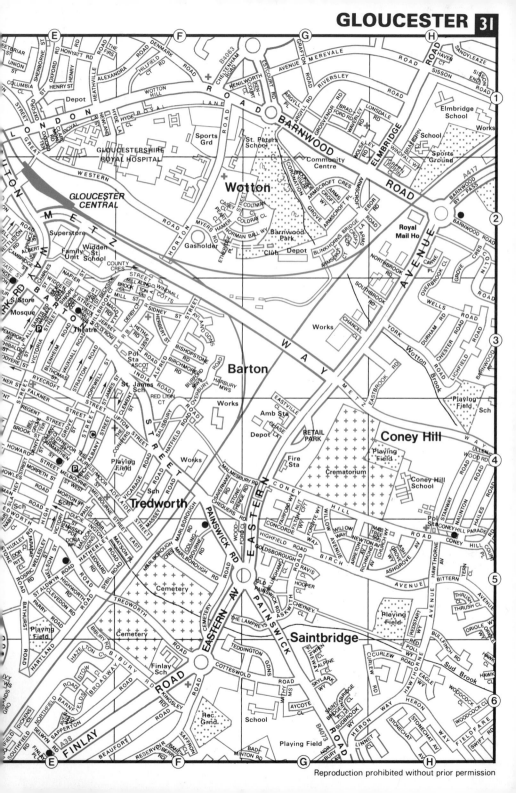

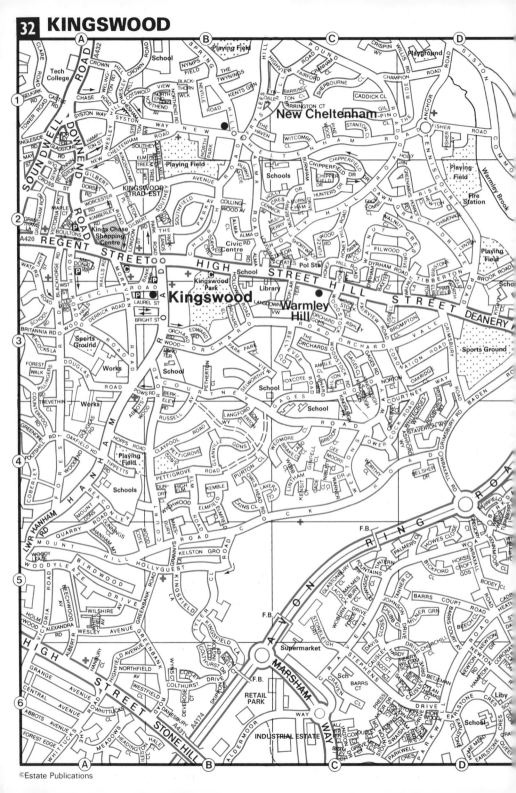

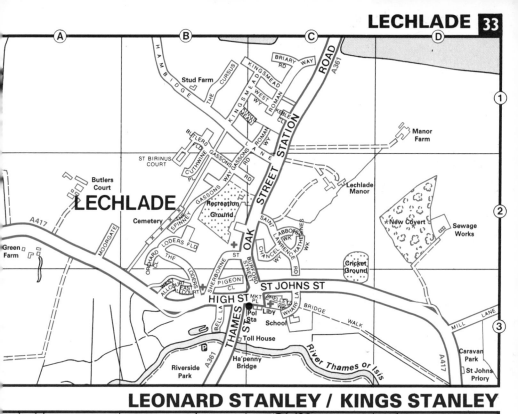

LECHLADE

LEONARD STANLEY / KINGS STANLEY

LEONARD STANLEY

KINGS STANLEY

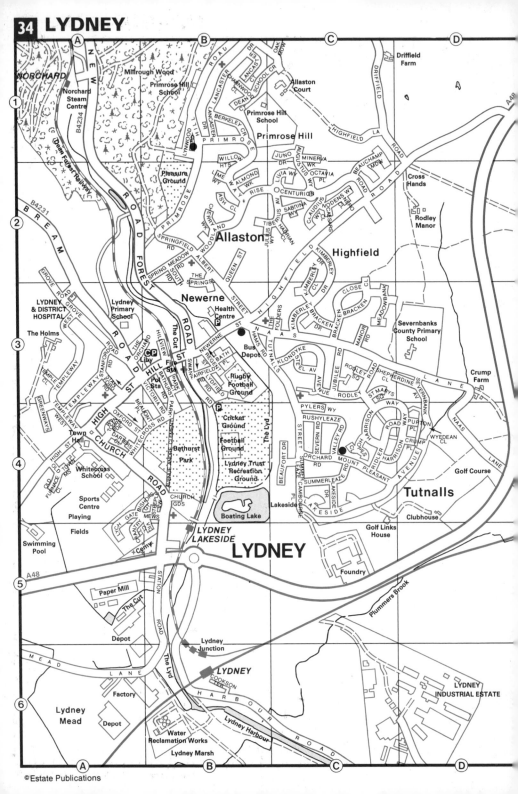

34 LYDNEY

©Estate Publications

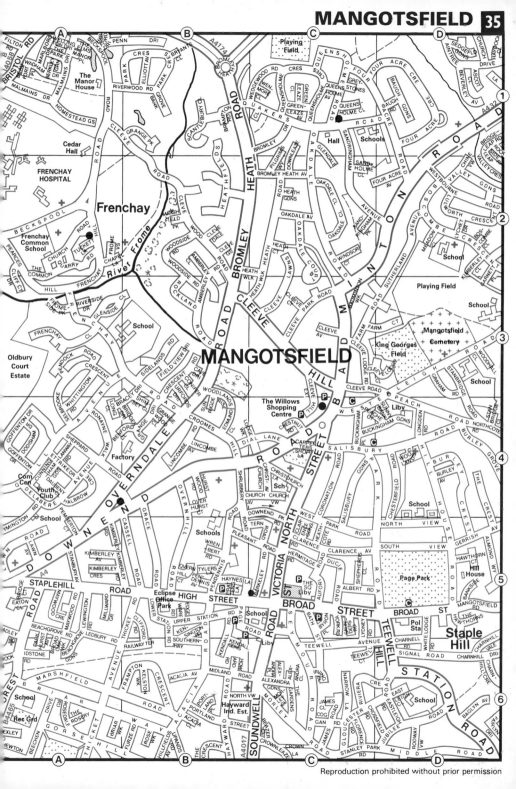

MANGOTSFIELD

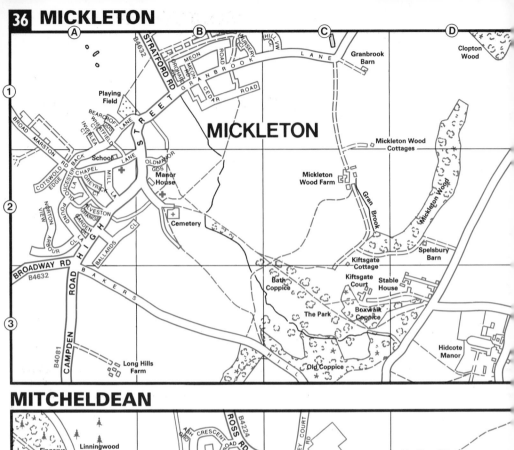

MICKLETON

MITCHELDEAN

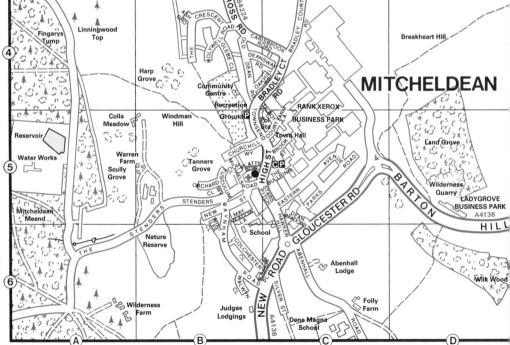

MITCHELDEAN

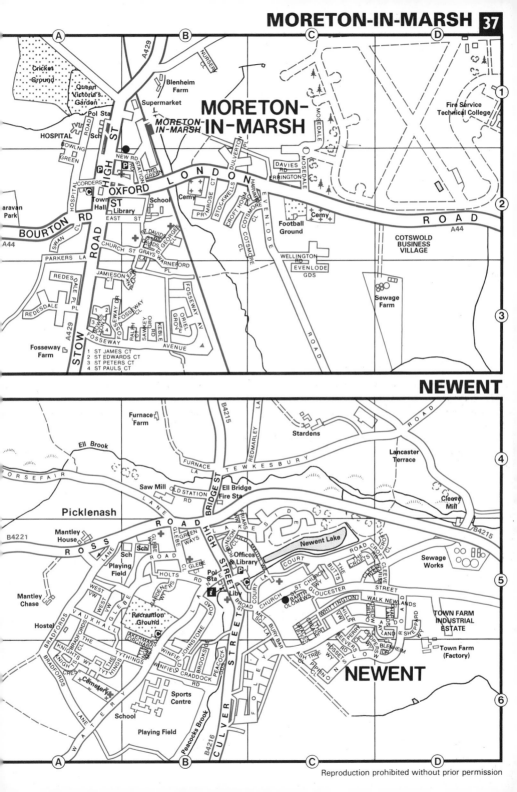

MORETON-IN-MARSH

NEWENT

1 ST JAMES CT
2 ST EDWARDS CT
3 ST PETERS CT
4 ST PAULS CT

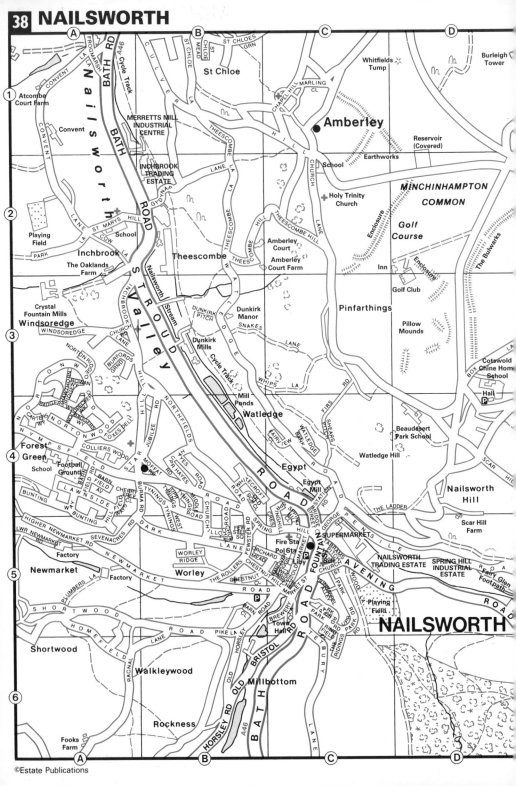

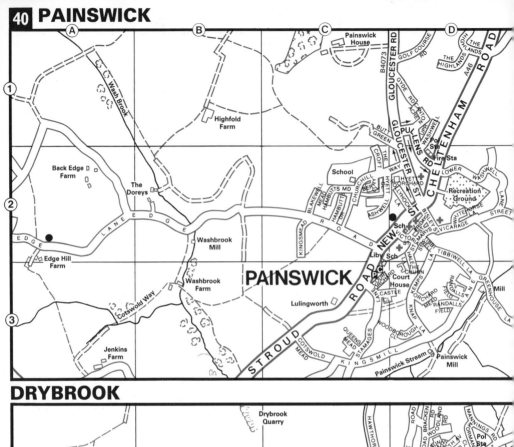

PAINSWICK

DRYBROOK

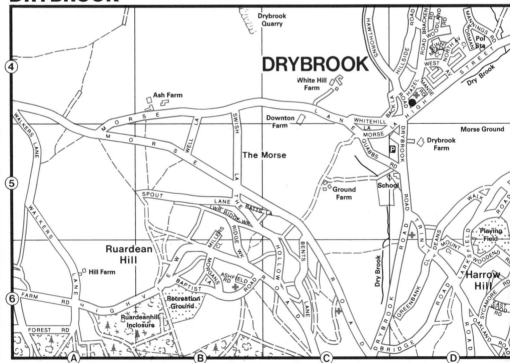

DRYBROOK

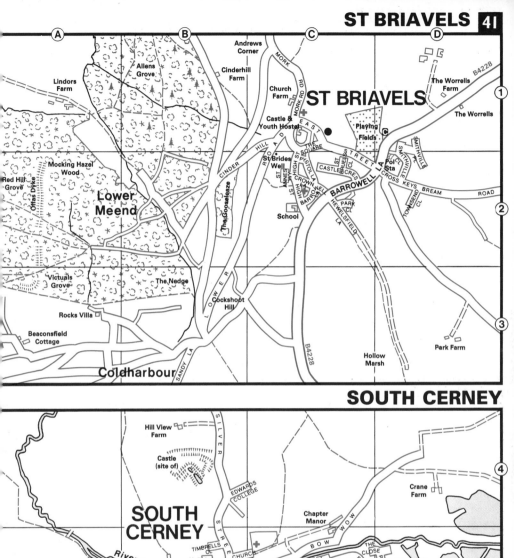

ST BRIAVELS

Andrews Corner
Cinderhill Farm
Allens Grove
Lindors Farm
Church Farm
The Worrells Farm
The Worrells
Castle & Youth Hostel
Playing Fields
Mocking Hazel Wood
Red Hill Grove
Offas Dyke
Lower Meend
The Gooseleaze
St Brides Well
BARROWELL
School
SMITHVILLE
CROSS KEYS
BREAM ROAD
TOWNSEND CL
Pol Sta
Victuals Grove
The Nedge
Rocks Villa
Cockshoot Hill
Beaconsfield Cottage
Coldharbour
Hollow Marsh
Park Farm

SOUTH CERNEY

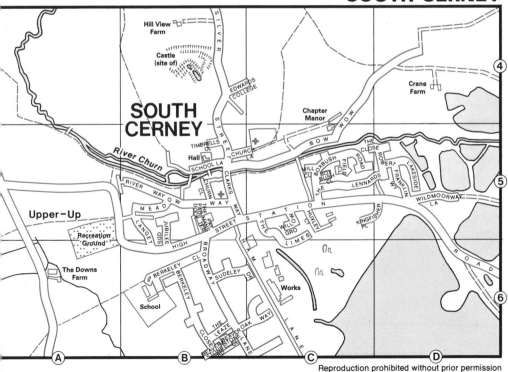

Hill View Farm
Castle (site of)
SILVER STREET
EDWARDS COLLEGE
Crane Farm
SOUTH CERNEY
Chapter Manor
River Churn
TIMBRELLS CL
Hall
CHURCH
BOW
THE CLOSE
MILL CL
BOXBUSH
FIELD ROAD
LAKESIDE
FRANKLIN
LENNARDS
WILDMOORWAY LA
SCHOOL LA
CLARKS WAY
THE LIMES
HUXLEY
WILLO GRO
KINGFISHER PL
Upper–Up
RIVER WAY
MEAD
LANGET
JUBILEE
HIGH
THE
DOWNS
STATION STREET
BROADWAY
Recreation Ground
The Downs Farm
BERKELEY CL
BERKELEY
SUDELEY DR
HAM LANE
Works
School
THE LEAZE
THE CLOSE
PRIMROSE
OAK WAY
LANE

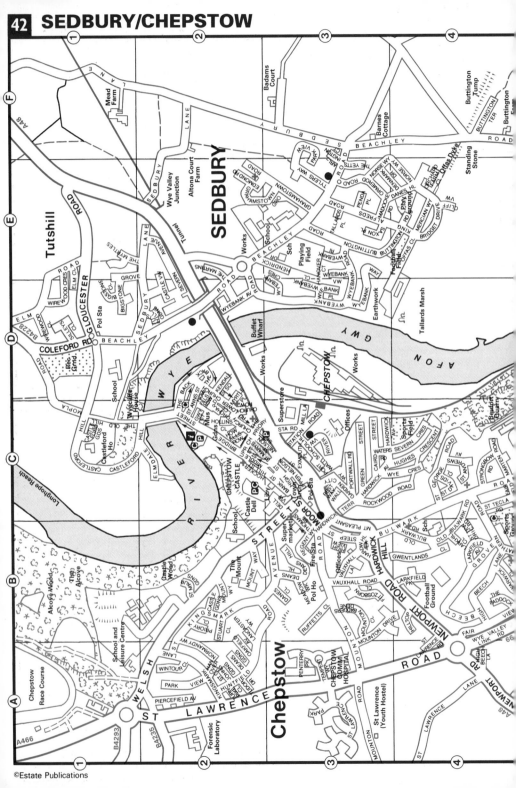

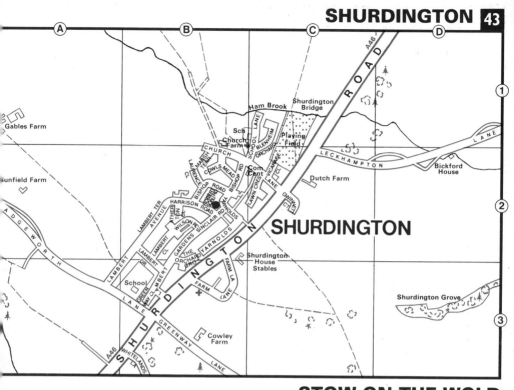

SHURDINGTON

STOW-ON-THE-WOLD

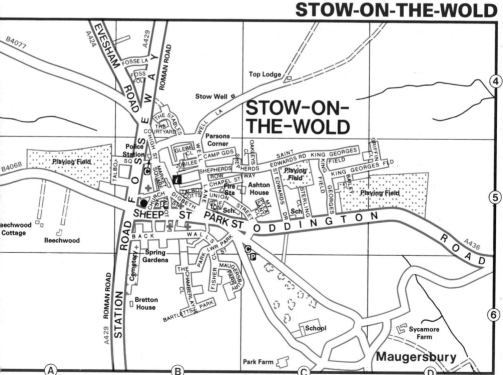

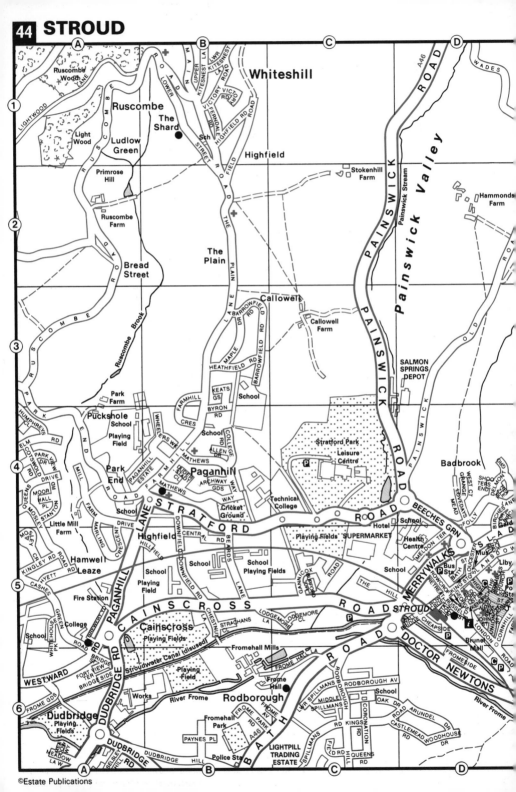

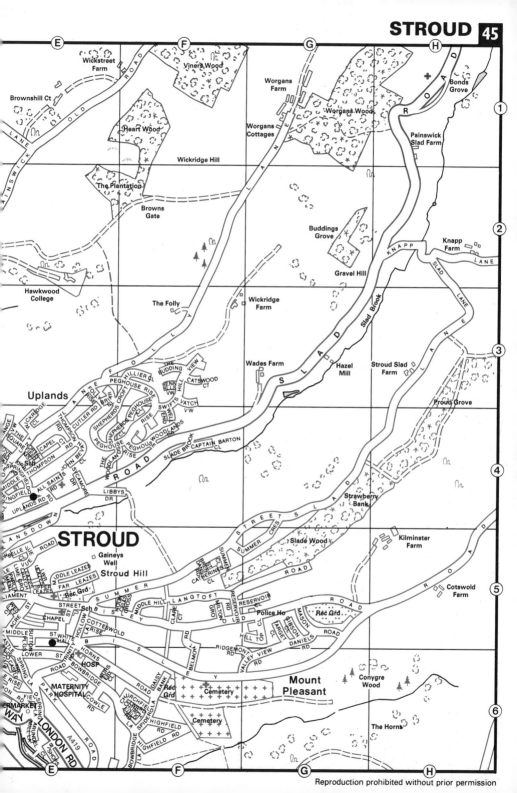

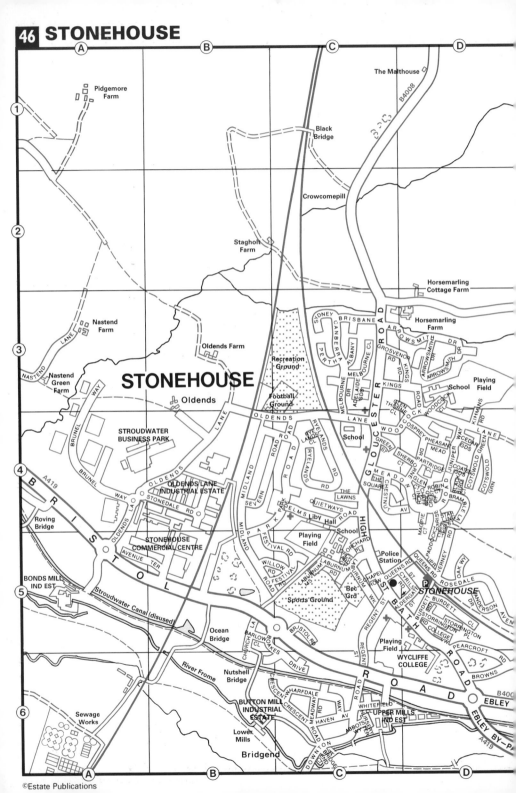

STONEHOUSE

Pidgemore Farm

The Malthouse

Black Bridge

Crowcomepill

Stagholt Farm

Horsemarling Cottage Farm

Horsemarling Farm

Nastend Farm

Oldends Farm

Recreation Ground

Playing Field

School

STONEHOUSE

Oldends

Football Ground

School

Nastend Green Farm

STROUDWATER BUSINESS PARK

OLDENDS

School

THE LAWNS

QUIETWAYS

Elms Liby Hall School

OLDENDS LANE INDUSTRIAL ESTATE

STONEHOUSE COMMERCIAL CENTRE

Playing Field

Police Station

STONEHOUSE

Roving Bridge

BONDS MILL IND EST

Stroudwater Canal (disused)

Sports Ground

Bet Grd

Playing Field

WYCLIFFE COLLEGE

Ocean Bridge

River Frome

Nutshell Bridge

BUTTON MILL INDUSTRIAL ESTATE

Sewage Works

Lower Mills

UPPER MILLS IND EST

EBLEY

Bridgend

EBLEY BY-P

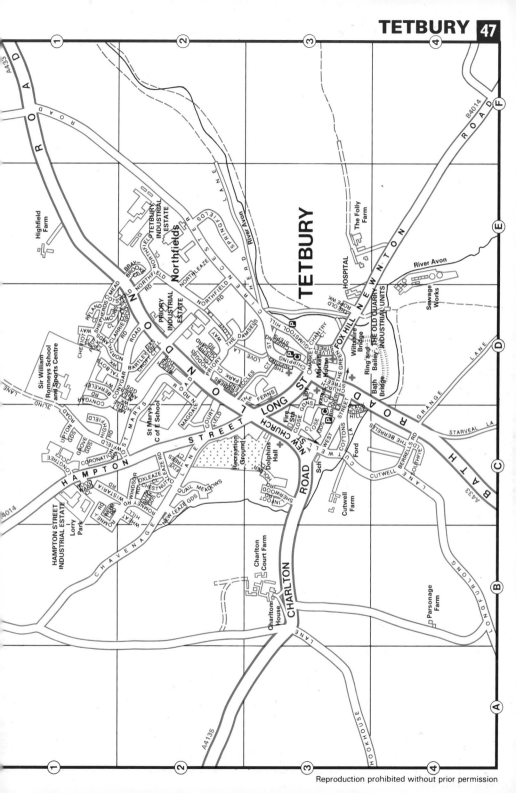

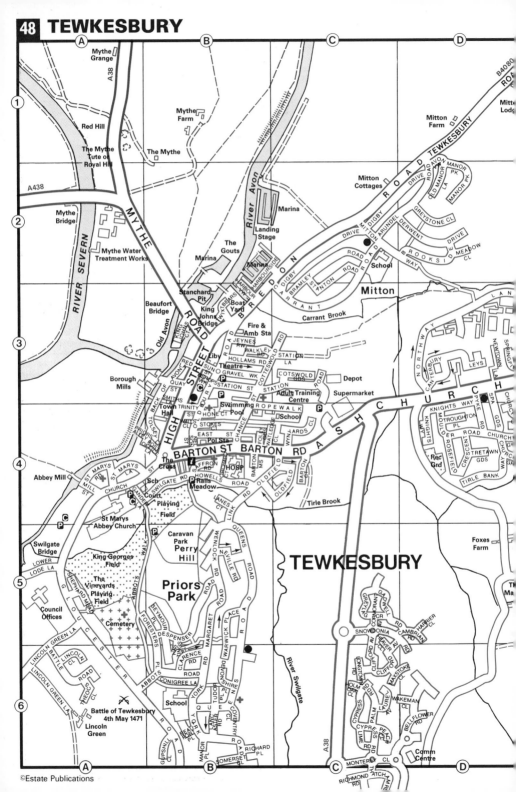

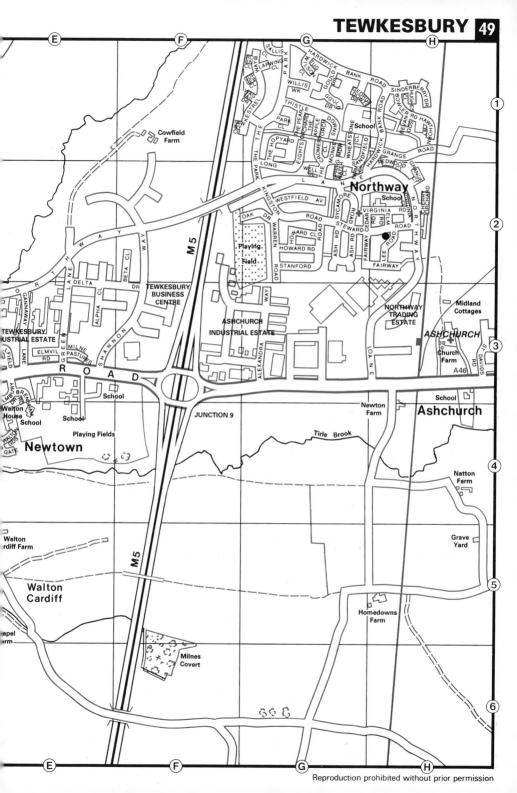

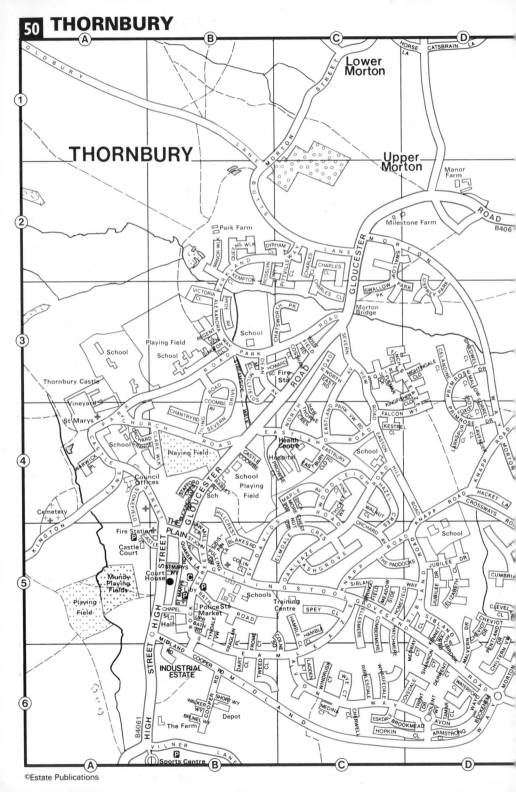

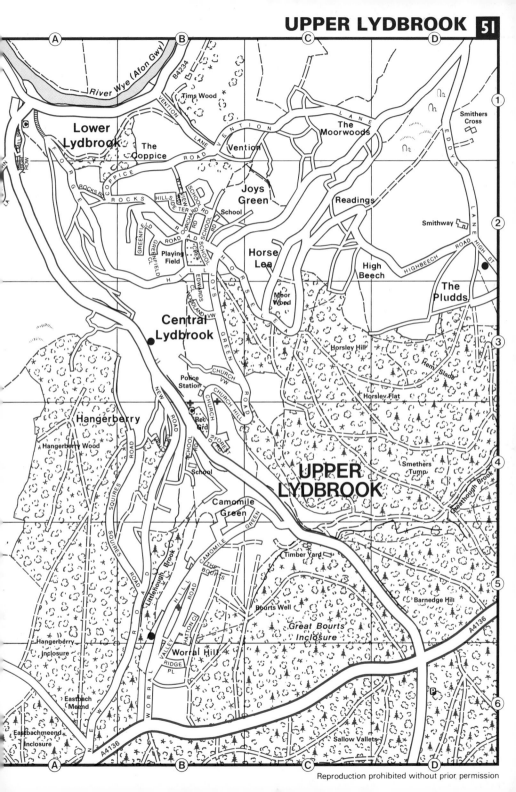

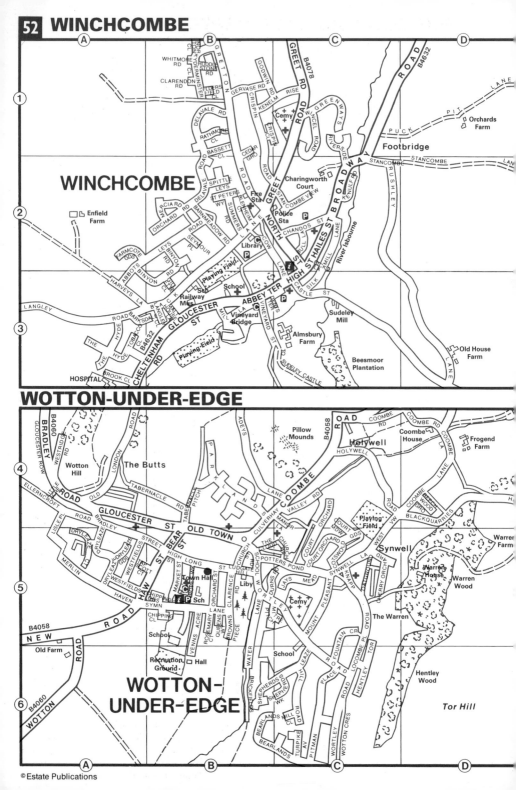

WINCHCOMBE

WOTTON-UNDER-EDGE

WOTTON-
UNDER-EDGE

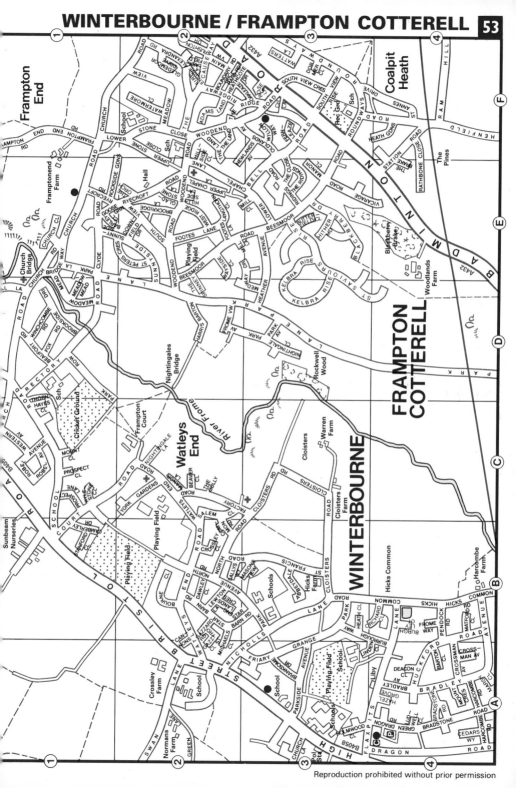

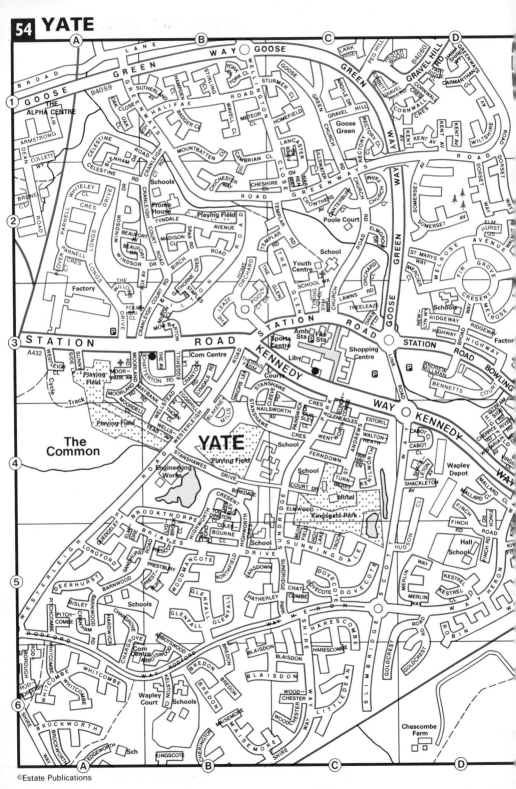

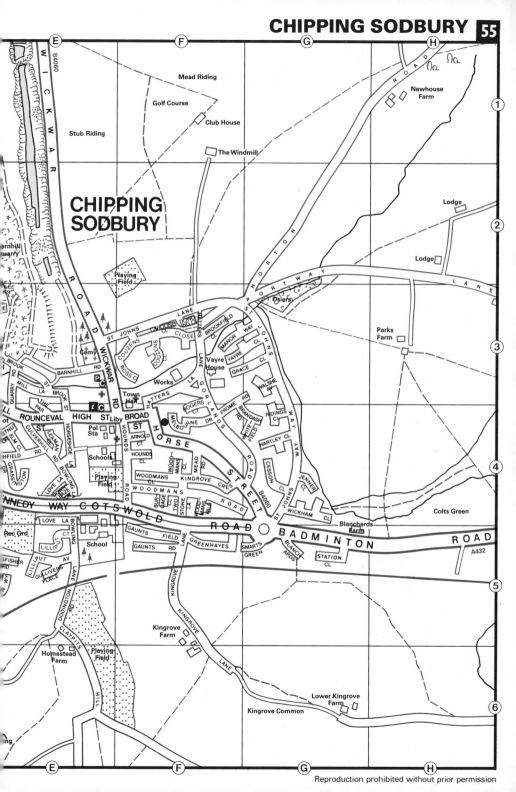

Mead Riding

Golf Course

Club House

Stub Riding

Newhouse Farm

The Windmill

CHIPPING SODBURY

Lodge

Barnhill Quarry

Lodge

Playing Field

Osiers

Parks Farm

St Johns Lane
Caroline Cl
Cozens
Ross Cl
Brookfield
Manor Way
St Johns
Cemy
Cozens Cl
Vayre House
Vayre
Grace Cl
Works
Walshe Av

Barnhill Rd
Wickwar Rd
Town Hall
Hatters La
Gorlands La
Frome Rd
Brandash Rd
Ridings Way
Whitefield
Hartley Cl

ROUNCEVAL ST   HIGH ST   Liby   BROAD ST
Rogers Cl
Melbourne Dr
Cesson Cl

Brook Rd
Mill La
Quarry La
The Par
Culverhill
Elm La
Horseshoe La
Pol Sta
Arnold Ct
Schools
Hounds
Hounds Cl
Woodmans Cl
Mead Rd
Kingrove Cres
Jenner Cl

HORSE STREET
Bowling La
Love La
Grassmere Dr
Playing Field
Woodmans Cl
Woodmans Road
Burl Stone
Two
Woodmans Mead
Wickham Cl

NNEDY WAY   COTSWOLD   ROAD
Rec Grd
Love La
Bowling Ct
Lilly Ct
School
Gaunts Field
Gaunts Rd
Greenhayes
Smarts Green
Blanchards
Colts Green

BADMINTON   ROAD
A432

Lillip Put Av
Gullivers Place
Kingrove La
Blanchards Cl
Station Cl
Blanchards Farm

Doddington Rd
Claypits
Kingrove La
Kingrove Farm

Homestead Farm
Playing Field

Lower Kingrove Farm
Kingrove Common

HILL

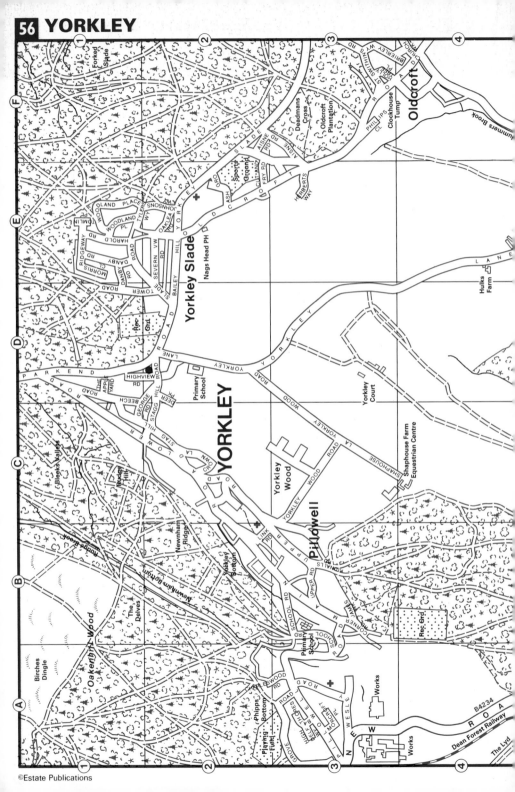

A - Z INDEX TO STREETS
with Postcodes

The Index includes some names for which there is insufficient space on the maps. These names are preceded by an * and are followed by the nearest adjoining thoroughfare.

ALMONDSBURY/ PATCHWAY

Amberley Rd. BS34 13 D5
Apex Ct. BS32 12 F3
Apsleys Mead. BS32 12 E4
Arlingham Way. BS34 13 A5
Ash Clo. BS34 13 F7
Ash Ridge Rd. BS32 12 D3
Ashford Rd. BS34 13 C6
Atwell Dri. BS32 12 D4
Badgers Clo. BS32 12 F3
Baytree Rd. BS34 13 B6
Beaufort Pk. BS32 12 F3
Bevington Clo. BS34 13 A5
Bevington Wk. BS34 13 A5
Bibury Av. BS34 13 D6
Birch Clo. BS34 13 A7
Blackthorn Dri. BS32 13 F6
Blakeney Rd. BS34 13 A5
Bourland Clo. BS32 12 F4
Bourton Av. BS34 13 E5
Bourton Clo. BS34 13 E6
Bowsland Way. BS32 12 E4
Brackendean. BS32 12 E4
Bradley Rd. BS34 13 A6
Bradley Stoke Way. BS32 12 D4
Brighton Rd. BS34 13 B6
Broad Croft. BS32 12 E4
Brockley Clo. BS34 13 E7
Brook Way. BS32 12 E4
Brookcote Dri. BS34 13 F8
Brookfield Rd. BS34 13 D6
Brotherwood Ct. BS32 12 F3
Bullens Clo. BS32 12 F4
Bush Av. BS34 13 E8
Callicroft Rd. BS34 13 C6
Campion Dri. BS32 12 F4
Carter Walk. BS32 13 F6
Cavendish Rd. BS34 13 B6
Cedar Clo. BS34 13 B7
Chalcombe Clo. BS34 13 E6
Chelford Gdns. BS34 13 D6
Chessel Clo. BS32 12 E4
Chestermaster Clo. BS32 12 C1
Church Rd. BS32 12 C1
Clay La. BS34 13 D6
Clover Lease. BS32 13 F8
Coleridge Ho. BS34 13 C5
Collins Av. BS34 13 E7
Concorde Rd. BS34 13 A7
Coniston Rd. BS34 13 A6
Cooks Clo. BS32 12 E3
Cope Park. BS32 12 E1
Cornfield Clo. BS32 13 E5
Court Vw Clo. BS32 12 C1
Cranbourne Rd. BS34 13 B6
Cranham Dri. BS34 13 E5
Crantock Dri. BS32 12 D1
Crofters Wk. BS32 13 F6
Cross Tree Gro. BS32 13 F6
Crows Grove. BS32 12 F3
Derwent Clo. BS34 13 C6
Dewfalls Dri. BS32 13 F5
Durban Rd. BS34 13 C6
Dyrham Av. BS34 13 E6
Eagle Dri. BS34 13 A6
Elm Clo. BS34 13 F7
Elmore Rd. BS34 13 B5
Elms Gro. BS34 13 D5
Epney Clo. BS34 13 B5
Fairford Cres. BS34 13 D6
Falcon Dri. BS34 13 A6
Falcon Wk. BS34 13 A5
Farley Clo. BS34 13 E6
Fern Gro. BS32 13 F6
Ferndean. BS32 12 E4
Filby Dri. BS34 13 E6
Firtree Clo. BS34 13 B7
Florence Park. BS32 12 D1
Forest Hills. BS32 12 D1
Foxborough Gdns. BS32 12 F4
Foxfield Av. BS32 12 F3
Gallivan Clo. BS34 13 D6
Gipsy Patch La. BS34 13 D8
Gloucester Rd. BS34 13 C8
Gloucester Rd. BS32 12 D2
Grange Av. BS34 13 E7
Grange Clo. BS32 12 E4
Great Park Rd. BS32 12 E3
Hallow Rd. BS32 12 C2
Harvest Clo. BS32 13 E5
Hatchet Rd. BS34 13 F8
Hawkins Cres. BS32 13 F6
Hawkesley Dri. BS34 13 F8
Hawkley Dri. BS32 12 F3
Hawthorn Clo. BS34 13 A6
Hazeldene Rd. BS34 13 C7
Hempton La. BS32 12 C4
Hercules Clo. BS34 13 F7
Highnam Clo. BS34 13 D5
Highwood La. BS34 13 A7
Highwood Rd. BS34 13 A7
Hortham La. BS32 12 F1
INDUSTRIAL & RETAIL:
Almondsbury Business Centre. BS32 12 E2
Eagles Wood Business Park. BS32 12 E3
Great Park. BS32 12 E3
Orpen Park Business Park. BS32 12 D3
Patchway Trading Estate. BS34 13 A6
Quadrant Business Centre. BS32 12 D3
The Grove Ind Est. BS32 13 D6
The Mall Regional Shopping Centre. BS34 13 A8
Jordan Wk. BS32 13 F6
Kemperleye Way. BS32 13 F6
Kestrel Clo. BS34 13 A6
Kilminster Clo. BS34 13 F7
Kingsway. BS34 13 E8
Kites Clo. BS32 12 E4
Knole Clo. BS32 12 B2
Knole Park. BS32 12 B3
Lamb Ho. BS34 13 C5
Lapwing Clo. BS32 12 F4
Larch Way. BS34 13 A7
Lawford Av. BS34 13 E8
Lee Clo. BS34 13 B6
Lime Kiln. BS32 12 F3
Linnet Clo. BS34 13 A6
Little Stoke La. BS34 13 E7
Littleton Ct. BS34 13 B5
Longney Pl. BS34 13 B5
Lower Court Rd. BS32 12 C1
Maismore Av. BS34 13 D5
Mallard Clo. BS32 12 F4
Maltravers Clo. BS32 13 F6
Manor Farm Cres. BS32 13 F5
Manor Gro. BS34 12 D4
Maple Clo. BS34 13 E7
Marshwood La. BS32 12 B1
Martin Clo. BS34 13 A6
Merryweather Clo. BS32 13 F6
Monmouth Hill. BS32 12 A2
Morley Clo. BS34 13 E6
New Leaze. BS32 12 E3
Newnham Pl. BS34 13 B5
Oak Clo. BS34 13 F7
Oak Tree Cres. BS32 12 D4
Oaklands Dri. BS32 12 C2
Old Aust La. BS32 12 E1
Olympus Clo. BS34 13 F8
Orion Dri. BS34 13 F8
Ormsley Clo. BS34 13 E6
Orpheus Av. BS34 13 F8
Ottrells Mead. BS32 12 E3
Over La. BS32 12 A4
Painswick Av. BS34 13 D6
Park Av. BS32 12 C4
Park Leaze. BS34 13 A5
Pear Tree Rd. BS32 12 E4
Penrose Dri. BS32 13 F6
Pretoria Rd. BS34 13 B5
Primrose Clo. BS32 12 F4
Queensway. BS34 13 E8
Ravenscourt Rd. BS34 13 D7
Redfield Rd. BS34 13 D7
Redhouse La. BS32 12 D2
Rodway Rd. BS34 13 B6
Rossall Av. BS34 13 E7
Rudford Clo. BS34 13 D5
Rush Clo. BS32 12 F4
Ruskin Ho. BS34 13 C6
Sandhurst Clo. BS34 13 D5
Savage Wood Rd. BS32 13 F6
School Clo. BS34 13 E6
Severn Way. BS34 13 B5
Sheils Dri. BS32 13 F7
Shelley Ho. BS34 13 C5
Shellmor Av. BS34 13 D5
Shellmor Clo. BS34 13 E5
Silverbirch Clo. BS34 13 F7
Silver Brook. BS32 13 F7
Smithcourt Dri. BS34 13 E8
Somerby Clo. BS32 13 F7
Southsea Rd. BS34 13 C6
Spruce Way. BS34 13 A7
Standish Av. BS34 13 D5
Stanshaws Clo. BS32 12 E4
Station Rd. BS34 13 D6
Staverton Way. BS34 13 D5
Stean Bridge Rd. BS32 13 F8
Stevens Wk. BS32 13 F6
Stoke Bridge Av. BS34 13 F8
Stoke La. BS34 13 D5
Stoke Mead. BS34 13 E6
Stoke Mdws. BS32 13 F5
Stratton Clo. BS34 13 E6
Stroud Rd. BS34 13 A6
Sundays Hill. BS32 12 C2
Swallow Dri. BS34 13 A6
Sycamore Dri. BS34 13 A7
Teal Clo. BS32 12 F4
Tetbury Clo. BS34 13 E6
The Avenue, Little Stoke. BS34 13 E8
The Avenue, Patchway. BS34 12 D4
The Beeches. BS32 13 F6
The Close, Little Stoke. BS34 13 E8
The Close, Patchway. BS34 12 E4
The Common. BS34 13 D5
The Common East. BS34 13 E5
The Courtyard. BS32 12 F3
The Culvert. BS32 13 F6
The Grove. BS34 13 D6
The Hill. BS32 12 D2
The Park. BS32 12 E3
The Pound. BS32 12 C1
The Quarries. BS32 12 D1
The Scop. BS32 12 C1
The Sherrings. BS34 13 D6
The Willows. BS32 13 F6
Thirlmere Rd. BS34 13 C6
Tidenham Way. BS34 13 B5
Tockington La. BS32 12 C1
Townsend La. BS32 12 B2
Trench La. BS32 12 F3
Tresham Clo. BS32 12 F4
Walnut Tree Clo. BS32 12 C1
Warren Clo. BS32 12 F3
Waterside Dri. BS32 13 C5
West Point Row. BS32 12 E3
Westfield Way. BS32 12 F3
Wheatfield Dri. BS32 13 F5
Willow Clo. BS34 13 A7
Windermere Rd. BS34 13 C6
Woodlands. BS32 12 F3
Woodlands La. BS32 12 D4
Wordsworth Ho. BS34 13 C5
Worthing Rd. BS34 13 B6
Wrington Clo. BS34 13 E6
Wroxham Dri. BS34 13 E6

BERKELEY

Berkeley By-Pass. GL13 14 C1
Berrycroft. GL13 14 C1
Cannonbury St. GL13 14 C2
Canon Park. GL13 14 C1
Church La. GL13 14 C2
Coach Clo. GL13 14 B2
Fishers Rd. GL13 14 B1
Fitzhardinge Way. GL13 14 B1
Forrest View Rd. GL13 14 B1
Gilbert Hill. GL13 14 B1
Hamfield La. GL13 14 A2
High St. GL13 14 C2
Hillcrest. GL13 14 C2
Hook La. GL13 14 D2
Howmead. GL13 14 B1
James Orchard. GL13 14 B2
Jenner Ct. GL13 14 B2
Jumpers La. GL13 14 B2
Lantern Clo. GL13 14 B2
Leaze Clo. GL13 14 B2
Lower Berrycroft. GL13 14 C2
Lynch Rd. GL13 14 A1
Marybrook St. GL13 14 C2
Park View Rd. GL13 14 B2
Salter St. GL13 14 B2
Severn Dri. GL13 14 B1
Station Rd. GL13 14 C1
Stock La. GL13 14 B2
The Brambles. GL13 14 C1
The Leys. GL13 14 C2
Trevisa Cres. GL13 14 C2

BISHOPS CLEEVE

Abbots Mws. GL52 15 B4
Acacia Pk. GL52 15 A2
Aesops Orchard. GL52 15 F2
Alverton Dri. GL52 15 B4
Anderson Clo. GL52 15 E3
Apple Tree Clo. GL52 15 F3
Ashfield Clo. GL52 15 D3
Ashlea Mdws. GL52 15 A2
Barker Leys. GL52 15 D2
Beechurst Way. GL52 15 A2
Berwick Rd. GL52 15 C1
Beverley Gdns. GL52 15 F3
Birchfield Rd. GL52 15 D2
Bishops Cleeve By-Pass. GL52 15 B2
Bishops Clo. GL52 15 D3
Bishops Dri. GL52 15 C3
Bishops Mdw. GL52 15 B2
Blackberry Gro. GL52 15 B2
Bootenhay Rd. GL52 15 D2
Bramble Chase. GL52 15 B2
Bregawn Clo. GL52 15 B4
Britannia Way. GL52 15 E2
Buckland Clo. GL52 15 C2
Bushcombe Clo. GL52 15 F2
Bushcombe La. GL52 15 F2
Butts La. GL52 15 E1
Byfield Clo. GL52 15 F3
Cantors Ct. GL52 15 C4
Cantors Dri. GL52 15 B4
Cares Clo. GL52 15 D2
Celandine Bank. GL52 15 E2
Chandler Rd. GL52 15 C4
Chantry Gate. GL52 15 B4
Chapel La. GL52 15 F3
Charlcote Corner. GL52 15 B3
Cheltenham Rd. GL52 15 C4
Chiltern Av. GL52 15 B2
Church Rd. GL52 15 C2
Churchfields. GL52 15 D2
Cleeve Ct. GL52 15 C3
Cleeve Lake Ct. GL52 15 B2
Cleevecroft Av. GL52 15 D3
Clematis Ct. GL52 15 B3
Coombe Meade. GL52 15 E3
Cornfield Dri. GL52 15 B2
Cotswold Vw. GL52 15 E3
Courtiers Dri. GL52 15 D3
Cowslip Meadow. GL52 15 E3
Cranford Clo. GL52 15 F3
Crowfield. GL52 15 E2
Crown Clo. GL52 15 C3
Crown Dri. GL52 15 C3
Cutsdean Clo. GL52 15 A2
Dale Walk. GL52 15 D3
Deacons Pl. GL52 15 B4
Deans Way. GL52 15 C3
Delabere Rd. GL52 15 D4
Delphinium Dri. GL52 15 B3
Denham Clo. GL52 15 F3
Denley Clo. GL52 15 C3
Dewey Clo. GL52 15 E3
East Gable. GL52 15 F3
Ellenborough Rd. GL52 15 D4
Evesham Rd. GL52 15 C1
Farriers Reach. GL52 15 A2
Fieldgate Rd. GL52 15 D2
Foster Clo. GL52 15 D1
Fox Moor. GL52 15 B2
Furlong La. GL52 15 C3
Gable Point. GL52 15 E3
Gambles La. GL52 15 F3
Gatcombe Clo. GL52 15 B3
Gilder Rd. GL52 15 D4
Gilders Paddock. GL52 15 C2
Gotherington La. GL52 15 D2
Grange Dri. GL52 15 C3
Green Meadow Bank. GL52 15 B2
Greenway. GL52 15 E3
Hardy Rd. GL52 15 C2
Harpfield Clo. GL52 15 C3
Harpfield Rd. GL52 15 C3
Harvesters Vw. GL52 15 A2
Hawthorn Dri. GL52 15 E3
Haycroft Clo. GL52 15 B2
Hayfield Way. GL52 15 A1
Haylea Rd. GL52 15 A2
Hemming Way. GL52 15 C3
Hertford Rd. GL52 15 D2
Hillside Clo. GL52 15 F3
Hillside Gdns. GL52 15 F3
Hisnams Field. GL52 15 C3
Holder Rd. GL52 15 C4
Honeysuckle Way. GL52 15 B1
Hunters Rd. GL52 15 B2
Huntsmans Clo. GL52 15 D2
Huxley Way. GL52 15 A2
Hyatts Way. GL52 15 D3
Icombe Clo. GL52 15 C3
INDUSTRIAL & RETAIL:
Cleeve Business Pk. GL52 15 B4
Jardine Dri. GL52 15 B2
Jesson Rd. GL52 15 D3
Kayte Clo. GL52 15 C4
Kayte La. GL52 15 D3
Keepers Mill. GL52 15 E3
Kempsford Acre. GL52 15 E3
Kingsclere Dri. GL52 15 B3
Kingswood Clo. GL52 15 C3
Lavender Ms. GL52 15 B3
Lears Dri. GL52 15 D3
Lindhurst Clo. GL52 15 E3
Lindley Chase. GL52 15 A2
Linworth Rd. GL52 15 D3
Little Acorns. GL52 15 B1
Little Orchard. GL52 15 B2
Littlecote Clo. GL52 15 B3
Longlands Clo. GL52 15 E2
Longlands La. GL52 15 D3
Marlborough Clo. GL52 15 B3
Mayfield Clo. GL52 15 C4
Meade King Gro. GL52 15 E3
Meadow Lea. GL52 15 B4
Meadoway. GL52 15 B4
Meads Clo. GL52 15 D3
Middle Hay Ct. GL52 15 B3
Millham Rd. GL52 15 D2
Minetts Av. GL52 15 D3
Minster Clo. GL52 15 B2
Moreton Clo. GL52 15 D4
Murray Clo. GL52 15 C2
New Rd. GL52 15 F3
Nortenham Clo. GL52 15 A2
Nottingham Rd. GL52 15 C1
Oakfield Rd. GL52 15 D3
Old Acre Dri. GL52 15 D1
Orchard Rd. GL52 15 C3
Owls End Rd. GL52 15 D2
Oxmead Clo. GL52 15 E2
Pagets Rd. GL52 15 D3
Pear Tree La. GL52 15 F3
Pecked La. GL52 15 D2
Pine Bank. GL52 15 E2
Poplar Ct. GL52 15 F3
Potters Field Rd. GL52 15 F3
Priory La. GL52 15 D2
Pullar Clo. GL52 15 C2
Pullar Ct. GL52 15 C2

Read Way. GL52 15 C4
Roberts Clo. GL52 15 C2
Rosehip Way. GL52 15 C2
St Johns Clo. GL52 15 C2
St Michaels Av. GL52 15 D3
Sandown Rd. GL52 15 C2
School Rd. GL52 15 D2
Sedgley Rd. GL52 15 C2
Selbourne Rd. GL52 15 C2
Shipway Ct. GL52 15 C2
Snowshill Dri. GL52 15 B3
Station Rd. GL52 15 C2
Stella Way. GL52 15 A2
Stockwell La. GL52 15 F3
Stoke Orchard Rd. GL52 15 A2
Stoke Park Clo. GL52 15 B2
Stoke Park Ct. GL52 15 B2
Stoke Rd. GL52 15 A2
Stonecroft Clo. GL52 15 B2
Streamside. GL52 15 C2
Sunnycroft Clo. GL52 15 D3
Sweetbriar Clo. GL52 15 D3
Thatchers End. GL52 15 E3
The Cloisters. GL52 15 B2
The Cornfields. GL52 15 A2
The Highgrove. GL52 15 B3
The Holt. GL52 15 B3
The Nurseries. GL52 15 B4
The Rowans. GL52 15 E3
The Withers. GL52 15 C2
Tobyfield Clo. GL52 15 D3
Tobyfield La. GL52 15 D2
Tobyfield Rd. GL52 15 D2
Two Hedges Rd. GL52 15 C3
Vilverie Mead. GL52 15 A2
Voxwell La. GL52 15 B3
Ward Clo. GL52 15 D2
Wellbrook Rd. GL52 15 C1
Wheatsheaf Dri. GL52 15 A2
Whitefields. GL52 15 A2
Whitehouse Way. GL52 15 E3
Willcox Dri. GL52 15 E3
Willow Clo. GL52 15 E3
Willow Park Dri. GL52 15 C2
Withyfield Rd. GL52 15 D2
Woodmancote Vale. GL52 15 E2
Wood Stanway Dri. GL52 15 B2
Woodmans Way. GL52 15 C3
Yarlington Clo. GL52 15 B2

BLAKENEY

All Saints Rd. GL15 14 D4
Awre Rd. GL15 14 D5
Blakeney Hill Rd. GL15 14 A5
Bridge St. GL15 14 C5
Butlers Mead. GL15 14 D5
Butts La. GL15 14 D5
Chapel Rd. GL15 14 A6
Church Sq. GL15 14 D5
Church Walk. GL15 14 A6
Church Way. GL15 14 D5
Cinderford Rd. GL15 14 C4
Clarks La. GL15 14 C4
Furnace Valley. GL15 14 B5
High St. GL15 14 C5
Highfield. GL15 14 C5
Loiterpin. GL15 14 C4
Meadow Clo. GL15 14 A6
Mill End. GL15 14 D5
New Rd. GL15 14 C5
Orchard Gate. GL15 14 C5
Pigeon Green. GL15 14 A5
Pine Tree Way. GL15 14 A6
Pollards La. GL15 14 B6
The Smithy. GL15 14 B6
Viney Woodside. GL15 14 B6

BOURTON-ON-THE-WATER

Baines Clo. GL54 16 B3
Beddome Way. GL54 16 C1
Bow La. GL54 16 C3
Broadlands Ct. GL54 16 C3
Cemetery La. GL54 16 D3
Chardwar Gdns. GL54 16 C3
Clapton Row. GL54 16 C3
Dikler Clo. GL54 16 E4
Essex Pl. GL54 16 B1

Folly Field. GL54 16 C2
Fosse Way. GL54 16 A3
Foxes Clo. GL54 16 C2
Gasworks La. GL54 16 C3
Gorse Clo. GL54 16 E4
Gorse Meadow. GL54 16 E4
Green La. GL54 16 B2
Greystones La. GL54 16 D2
High St. GL54 16 B2
Hilcote Dri. GL54 16 D4
INDUSTRIAL & RETAIL:
Bourton Ind Park. GL54 16 C1
Kings Meadow. GL54 16 C1
Lamberts Field. GL54 16 D3
Letch Hill Dri. GL54 16 A2
Letch La. GL54 16 C3
Marshmouth La. GL54 16 D4
Melville. GL54 16 C1
Moore La. GL54 16 D2
Moore Rd. GL54 16 C2
Mousetrap La. GL54 16 B2
Nethercote Dri. GL54 16 D4
Nethercote Farm Dri. GL54 16 D4
Old Gloucester Rd. GL54 16 A2
Park Farm. GL54 16 C1
Pegasus Ct. GL54 16 C2
Piece Hedge. GL54 16 C2
Pockhill La. GL54 16 B3
Rectory La. GL54 16 C2
Rissington Rd. GL54 16 C3
Roman Way. GL54 16 C2
Rye Clo. GL54 16 D3
Rye Cres. GL54 16 D3
Salmonsbury Cotts. GL54 16 C2
Sherborne St. GL54 16 B3
Springfield. GL54 16 B3
Springvale. GL54 16 C1
Station Meadow. GL54 16 C1
Station Rd. GL54 16 C1
The Avenue. GL54 16 C3
The Gorse. GL54 16 D4
The Naight. GL54 16 C3
Victoria St. GL54 16 C3

BREAM

Acacia Clo. GL15 17 D3
Badgers Way. GL15 17 D3
Beech Way. GL15 17 D3
Blue Rock Cres. GL15 17 D3
Bowson Rd. GL15 17 D1
Bowson Sq. GL15 17 D2
Bream Av. GL15 17 A3
Brockhollands Rd. GL15 17 D3
Coleford Rd. GL15 17 A3
Coxs Way. GL15 17 D2
Forest Rd. GL15 17 D2
Greenacre. GL15 17 D4
Hang Hill Rd. GL15 17 C2
Henley Rd. GL15 17 D2
High St. GL15 17 C3
Highbeech Rd. GL15 17 C3
Highbury Est. GL15 17 C3
Highbury Rd. GL15 17 C3
Highway Way. GL15 17 D3
Hillside Clo. GL15 17 D3
Hillside Est. GL15 17 C3
Ironstone Clo. GL15 17 C4
Knockley Patch. GL15 17 D1
Knox Rd. GL15 17 F4
Lansdown Walk. GL15 17 D3
Lydney Rd. GL15 17 C4
Maypole Green. GL15 17 C4
Montpelier Clo. GL15 17 E2
Montpelier Rd. GL15 17 E3
New Rd, Bream. GL15 17 B3
New Rd,
Whitecroft. GL15 17 F1
Oakley Rd. GL15 17 F2
Oakwood Rd. GL15 17 C2
Parawell La. GL15 17 A4
Park Gro. GL15 17 F2
Park Hill. GL15 17 F2
Parkend Rd. GL15 17 D1
Pastors Hill. GL15 17 D3
Pillowell Clo. GL15 17 F2
Pine Crest Way. GL15 17 C3
Puzzle Clo. GL15 17 C3
Ryelands Rd. GL15 17 D3
Sun Green Clo. GL15 17 C3

Sun Green Rd. GL15 17 C3
Sun Rise Rd. GL15 17 C2
Sun Tump. GL15 17 C3
The Tufts. GL15 17 B3
Trenchard Rd. GL15 17 D4
Whitechapel Rd. GL15 17 D2
Whitecroft Rd. GL15 17 D2
Whittington Way. GL15 17 D4
Woodland Rd. GL15 17 C2
Woodlands Clo. GL15 17 F2

BROCKWORTH

Abbotswood Rd. GL3 24 B6
Ansdell Dri. GL3 24 B4
Astor Clo. GL3 24 A4
Astridge Rd. GL3 24 D6
Avon Cres. GL3 24 C2
Boverton Av. GL3 24 B5
Boverton Dri. GL3 24 A4
Bryerland Rd. GL3 24 D3
Buckholt Way. GL3 24 B3
Castle Hill Dri. GL3 24 C6
Cedar Rd. GL3 24 A4
Chandos Dri. GL3 24 B6
Cirencester Rd. GL3 24 C6
Clyde Rd. GL3 24 B5
Coopers View. GL3 24 B6
Court Rd. GL3 24 A4
Derwent Clo. GL3 24 B5
Elm Dri. GL3 24 A4
Ermin Park. GL3 24 A4
Ermin St. GL3 24 A5
Fairhaven Av. GL3 24 B5
Gannet Clo. GL3 24 B6
Gladiator Clo. GL3 24 B6
Golf Club La. GL3 24 A5
Green Acre. GL3 24 B6
Green Bank. GL3 24 B6
Green Clo. GL3 24 B6
Green Gdns. GL3 24 B6
Green La. GL3 24 D4
Green St. GL3 24 A6
Green Way. GL3 24 B6
Guise Av. GL3 24 C6
Hebden Clo. GL3 24 C6
Hickley Gdns. GL3 24 B4
Hillview Av. GL3 24 A5
Humber Pl. GL3 24 C5
Hurcombe Way. GL3 24 B4
Javelin Way. GL3 24 B6
Lasne Cres. GL3 24 C6
Lea Rd. GL3 24 C5
Leadon Clo. GL3 24 C6
Maple Dri. GL3 24 A4
Medway Cres. GL3 24 C5
Meteor Way. GL3 24 B6
Mill Cnr. GL3 24 D6
Mill La. GL3 24 B5
Moorfield Rd. GL3 24 B5
Noak Rd. GL3 24 A4
Oak Dri. GL3 24 A5
Painswick Rd. GL3 24 C6
Pillcroft Clo. GL3 24 D6
Pillcroft Rd. GL3 24 D6
Pound Clo. GL3 24 B6
Ribble Clo. GL3 24 C5
Ridgemount Clo. GL3 24 B5
Rowan Gdns. GL3 24 A4
St Annes Clo. GL3 24 B5
St Georges Rd. GL3 24 B6
Sayers Cres. GL3 24 B5
Seabrook Rd. GL3 24 B6
Shurdington Rd. GL3 24 A5
Tamar Rd. GL3 24 C5
Tanners Clo. GL3 24 B4
The Crescent. GL3 24 A4
Theyer Clo. GL3 24 B6
Tone Dri. GL3 24 C6
Trent Rd. GL3 24 C5
Usk Way. GL3 24 C6
Vicarage La. GL3 24 B5
Westfield Av. GL3 24 A4
Westfield Rd. GL3 24 A5
Wye Rd. GL3 24 C6

CAM/DURSLEY

Acacia Dri. GL11 18 D4
Addymore. GL11 18 B3
April Clo. GL11 19 D7
Ash Clo. GL11 18 D4
Beechwood Rise. GL11 19 C6

Beyon Clo. GL11 18 B2
Beyon Dri. GL11 18 B2
Birch Rd. GL11 18 C4
Blackboys. GL11 19 C5
Blackwells. GL11 19 E8
Boulton La. GL11 19 D7
Bowers Lea. GL11 18 B2
Bramble Dri. GL11 18 C4
Broadmere. GL11 18 A4
Broadmere Clo. GL11 18 A4
Broadwell. GL11 19 E7
Broadwell Ter. GL11 19 E7
Bull Pitch. GL11 19 E7
Burnt Oak. GL11 19 C6
Byron Rd. GL11 19 E8
Cam Green. GL11 18 E2
Cam Pitch. GL11 18 B3
Cambridge Av. GL11 19 E8
Castle St. GL11 19 D6
Cedar Dri. GL11 19 D6
Chapel St. GL11 18 C2
Church Rd. GL11 18 D4
Courthouse Gdns. GL11 18 C2
Delkin Rd. GL11 18 B3
Drake La. GL11 19 E6
Draycott Cres. GL11 18 B1
Dursley Rd. GL11 18 A4
Elm Lodge. GL11 18 D3
Elstub La. GL11 18 A3
Everlands. GL11 18 C3
Everside Clo. GL11 18 B1
Everside La. GL11 18 B1
Ewelme Rd. GL11 19 F7
Fairmead. GL11 18 C3
Ferney. GL11 19 E7
Field La. GL11 18 A2
First Av. GL11 19 E7
Five Acres. GL11 19 D7
Fort Fields. GL11 19 D7
Fort La. GL11 19 E7
Fourth Av. GL11 19 F7
Frederick Thomas Rd. GL11 18 B3
Ganzell La. GL11 19 F8
Glebe Clo. GL11 18 C3
Green St. GL11 18 E2
Hadley Rd. GL11 18 A3
Hague Av. GL11 18 B3
Halmore La. GL11 18 E1
Hardings Dri. GL11 19 D6
Henlow Rd. GL11 19 D7
Hermitage Dri. GL11 19 E8
Hicks Av. GL11 18 B3
High Furlong. GL11 18 B3
High St. GL11 18 C2
Highfields App. GL11 19 E7
Hill Clo. GL11 18 C3
Hill Rd. GL11 19 C7
Hill Top Vw. GL11 18 B3
Holywell Rd. GL11 18 C4
Hopton Rd. GL11 18 D3
Hunger Hill. GL11 19 D7
INDUSTRIAL ESTATES:
Draycott Business
Park. GL11 18 C1
Jubilee Av. GL11 18 B1
Jubilee Clo. GL11 18 B1
Jubilee Rd. GL11 19 C5
Kings Dri. GL11 19 C5
Kings Way. GL11 19 C5
Kingsdown. GL11 19 D5
Kingshill La. GL11 19 C5
Kingshill Park. GL11 19 C5
Kingshill Rd. GL11 19 C5
Kipling Rd. GL11 19 F8
Knapp La. GL11 18 B2
Lambsdowne. GL11 18 B4
Larkrise. GL11 18 B3
Lawrence Gro. GL11 19 C5
Leaside Clo. GL11 18 C3
Long St. GL11 19 D6
Lower Poole Rd. GL11 19 D7
Manor Av. GL11 18 B2
Manor Clo. GL11 18 B2
Maple Dri. GL11 18 D4
Marlestone Rd. GL11 18 C4
Marment Rd. GL11 18 A4
May Evans Clo. GL11 18 B3
May La. GL11 19 D7
Meadow Vale. GL11 18 B4
Mill Way. GL11 18 C3
Millbank. GL11 18 D3
Morris Orchard. GL11 18 B2
Nasse Ct. GL11 18 B2
New Rd. GL11 18 B4
Noel Lee Way. GL11 18 C2

Nordown Clo. GL11 18 C3
Nordown Rd. GL11 18 C3
Norman Hill. GL11 18 B3
Nunnery La. GL11 19 D8
Oak Dri. GL11 18 D4
Old Ct. GL11 19 E5
Olive Gro. GL11 19 C5
Orchard Clo. GL11 18 B4
Orchard Leaze. GL11 18 A4
Orchard Rise. GL11 18 C4
Park La. GL11 19 A8
Parkland Rd. GL11 18 C4
Parsonage St. GL11 19 D6
Pevelands. GL11 18 B2
Phillimore Rd. GL11 18 A4
Quarry Gdns. GL11 18 A4
Rangers Av. GL11 19 E8
Rednock Dri. GL11 19 C5
Reine Barnes Clo. GL11 19 E7
Rock Rd. GL11 18 A4
Rosebank. GL11 19 D6
Roseberry Mt. GL11 19 E7
Roseberry Park. GL11 19 E8
Roseberry Rd. GL11 19 E7
Rowan Gro. GL11 18 D4
Rowley. GL11 18 C2
Ryder Clo. GL11 18 C4
St Bartholomews Clo. GL11 18 B2
St Davids Cres. GL11 19 C5
St Georges Clo. GL11 18 D4
St Georges Rd. GL11 18 A3
School Clo. GL11 19 F7
Second Av. GL11 19 E7
Severn Rd. GL11 18 B4
Shakespeare Rd. GL11 19 F8
Shelley Rd. GL11 19 F8
Shutehay Dri. GL11 18 B2
Silver St. GL11 19 D7
Somerset Av. GL11 19 E8
Spark Hill. GL11 18 B2
Spouthouse La. GL11 18 C3
Springfield. GL11 18 B4
Springfield Ct. GL11 18 B4
Springhill. GL11 19 E5
Stanthill Dri. GL11 18 E7
Station Rd. GL11 18 C3
Steps Clo. GL11 18 B2
Stonelea. GL11 18 A4
Sutton Clo. GL11 19 D7
Taits Hill Rd. GL11 18 A4
Tennyson Rd. GL11 19 E8
The Avenue. GL11 18 A4
The Broadway. GL11 19 C7
The Close. GL11 18 B3
The Corriet. GL11 18 C3
The Crapen. GL11 18 A3
The Crescent. GL11 18 B3
The Croft. GL11 18 B3
The Drive. GL11 18 B3
The Hawthorns. GL11 18 B3
The Knapp. GL11 19 D6
The Quarry. GL11 18 A4
The Slade. GL11 19 D7
The Vennings. GL11 18 C3
Third Av. GL11 19 E7
Tilnor Cres. GL11 18 B3
Tilsdown. GL11 18 B3
Tilsdown Clo. GL11 18 B4
Tithe Ct. GL11 18 B2
Torchacre Rise. GL11 19 C6
Trotman Av. GL11 18 B3
Turner Rd. GL11 18 A3
Twinberrow La. GL11 19 E8
Tyndale Rd. GL11 18 A3
Uley Rd. GL11 19 E7
Union St. GL11 19 E7
Upper Poole Rd. GL11 19 D7
Upthorpe. GL11 18 B3
Upthorpe Dri. GL11 18 E2
Valley View. GL11 18 C3
Vizard Clo. GL11 19 E7
Water St. GL11 19 E6
Weavers Clo. GL11 19 D7
West End. GL11 18 A3
Westfield. GL11 19 C6
Whiteway. GL11 19 F8
Whiteway Clo. GL11 19 F8
Willow Clo. GL11 18 D4
Windsor Rd. GL11 19 D6
Withy Way. GL11 18 B3
Woodend La. GL11 18 A1
Woodfield Rd. GL11 18 A4
Woodland Av. GL11 19 C5
Woodland Dri. GL11 19 C6
Woodmancote. GL11 19 E7

Priory Pl. GL52 22 D6
Priory St. GL52 22 D6
Priory Ter. GL52 22 D6
Priory Walk. GL52 22 D6
Promenade. GL50 22 B6
Prospect Ter. GL52 22 D5
Purbeck Way. GL52 23 G3
Queen St. GL51 22 A4
Queens Retreat. GL51 22 A5
Queenwood Gro. GL52 23 H2
Red Rower Clo. GL50 22 B1
Regent St. GL50 22 C6
Richards Rd. GL51 22 A3
Richmond Dri. GL52 23 F5
Roberts Rd. GL52 23 H4
Robins Clo. GL52 23 E4
Rodney Rd. GL50 22 C6
Roman Hackle Av.
  GL50 22 B2
Roman Hackle Rd.
  GL50 22 B2
Rose & Crown Pass.
  GL50 22 C5
Royal Cres. GL50 22 C5
Royal Par Mews. GL50 22 B6
Royal Well La. GL50 22 B6
Royal Well Pl. GL50 22 B6
Royal Well Rd. GL50 22 C6
Rushy Mws. GL52 23 F3
Russell Pl. GL51 22 B4
Russell St. GL51 22 B4
Sackville App. GL50 22 C3
St Annes Clo. GL52 22 D5
St Annes Rd. GL52 22 D6
St Annes Ter. GL52 22 D6
St Arvens Ct. GL52 22 D3
St Georges Clo. GL51 22 A5
St Georges Dri. GL51 22 A5
St Georges Pl. GL50 22 B6
St Georges Rd. GL50 22 B6
St Georges St. GL50 22 C5
St James Sq. GL50 22 B5
St James St. GL52 22 D6
St Johns Av. GL52 22 D6
St Lukes Pl. GL52 22 C5
St Margarets Rd. GL50 22 C5
St Nicholas Dri. GL50 22 C2
St Pauls La. GL50 22 B4
St Pauls Rd. GL50 22 B4
St Pauls St Nth. GL50 22 C4
St Pauls St Sth. GL50 22 B5
Salamanca. GL52 23 G5
Sandford St. GL53 22 C6
Saville Clo. GL50 22 D3
Selkirk Clo. GL52 22 D4
Selkirk Gdns. GL52 22 D4
Selkirk St. GL52 22 D5
Seneca Way. GL50 22 A2
Seven Posts All. GL52 23 F3
Severn Rd. GL52 23 E4
Shaw Green La. GL52 23 F1
Sheldons Ct. GL52 22 D5
Sherborne Pl. GL52 22 D5
Sherborne St. GL52 22 D5
Sidney St. GL52 22 D6
Somme Rd. GL52 23 F4
South View Way. GL52 23 G3
Southam Rd. GL52 23 G1
Spring La. GL52 23 F1
Stanley Rd. GL52 23 F6
Stanwick Cres. GL51 22 A2
Stanwick Dri. GL51 22 A2
Stanwick Gdns. GL51 22 A3
Station St. GL50 22 B5
Stirling Ct. GL51 22 A1
Stoneville St. GL51 22 B4
Studland Dri. GL52 23 G3
Sun St. GL51 22 A4
Swindon Clo. GL51 22 B4
Swindon La. GL50 22 A1
Swindon Rd. GL51 22 B4
Swindon St. GL51 22 B4
Sydenham Rd Nth.
  GL52 23 E6
Sydenham Rd Sth.
  GL52 23 E6
Sydenham Villas Rd.
  GL52 22 D6
Tamar Rd. GL52 23 E4
Tatchley La. GL52 23 F3
Teme Rd. GL52 23 E5
Tewkesbury Rd. GL51 22 A3
Thames Rd. GL52 23 E4
The Bank. GL52 23 G2
The Burgage. GL52 23 F2
The Conifers. GL52 23 E4
The Gardens. GL50 22 D3

The Grove,
  Cheltenham. GL52 23 E6
The Grove,
  Lansdown. GL50 22 A6
The Gryphons. GL52 23 E5
The Spinney. GL52 22 D2
The Stables. GL52 23 H2
The Strand. GL50 22 C6
Thomond Clo. GL50 22 A2
Thornbury Co. GL51 22 A5
Three Sisters La. GL52 23 H3
Tilney Rd. GL51 22 C2
Tom Price Clo. GL52 22 D5
Tommy Taylors La.
  GL50 22 B3
Townsend St. GL51 22 B4
Trafalgar St. GL50 22 C6
Trinity La. GL52 22 C5
Trinity School La.
  GL52 22 D5
Union St. GL52 22 D5
Upper Mill La. GL52 23 H2
Vernon Pl. GL53 22 C6
Victoria Pl. GL52 22 D5
Victoria St. GL50 22 B4
Victoria Ter. GL52 23 E6
Vine Ct. GL50 22 B4
Vittoria Walk. GL50 22 C6
Waddon Dri. GL52 23 E4
Walnut Clo. GL54 22 D3
Warwick Pl. GL52 22 C5
Waterloo St. GL51 22 A3
Watershoot Clo. GL52 23 E2
Well Pl. GL50 22 A6
Welland Ct. GL52 23 E3
Welland Dri. GL52 23 E3
Welland Lodge Rd.
  GL52 23 E3
Wellesley Rd. GL50 22 C4
Wellington La. GL52 22 C4
Wellington Rd. GL52 22 D4
Wellington Sq. GL50 22 C4
Wellington St. GL50 22 C6
Wendover Gdns. GL50 22 A6
Wessex Dri. GL52 23 F5
West Approach Dri.
  GL52 22 D3
West Down Gdns.
  GL52 22 D5
West Dri. GL50 22 C4
Westbourne Dri. GL52 23 E5
Western Rd. GL50 22 A5
Westwood La. GL52 23 H4
Whaddon Av. GL52 23 E5
Whaddon Ct. GL52 23 E4
Whaddon Rd. GL52 23 E4
White Hart St. GL51 22 B4
Whitethorne Dri. GL52 23 G4
Willow Rd. GL53 23 F6
Willowherb Clo. GL52 23 G4
Winchcombe St. GL52 22 C5
Windrush Rd. GL52 23 F5
Windsor St. GL52 22 D4
Windyridge Gdns.
  GL50 22 B2
Windyridge Rd. GL50 22 A2
Winstonian Rd. GL52 22 D5
Witcombe Pl. GL52 22 D6
Worcester St. GL52 22 A3
Wymans La. GL51 22 A2
Wymans Rd. GL52 23 E4
Yew Tree Clo. GL52 22 B2
York Row. GL52 23 F3
York St. GL52 22 D5

CHIPPING CAMPDEN

Aston Rd. GL55 24 B1
Back Ends. GL55 24 B2
Badgers Field. GL55 24 B2
Berrington Rd. GL55 24 B2
Blind La. GL55 24 A3
Calfs La. GL55 24 B2
Castle Gdns. GL55 24 D2
Castle Nurseries. GL55 24 D2
Catbrook Clo. GL55 24 B3
Cherry Orchard Clo.
  GL55 24 B3
Church St. GL55 24 C2
Coldicotts Clo. GL55 24 B2
Conduit Hill. GL55 24 A3
Coneygree Fold. GL55 24 C1
Coronation Clo. GL55 24 A2

Dyers La. GL55 24 A2
George La. GL55 24 B3
Grafton Mews. GL55 24 B2
Grevel La. GL55 24 B1
Griggs Clo. GL55 24 B1
Haydens Clo. GL55 24 C1
Haysums Clo. GL55 24 B3
High St. GL55 24 B2
Hoo La. GL55 24 A2
Izods Clo. GL55 24 B3
Kingcombe La. GL55 24 A1
Leysbourne. GL55 24 B2
Littleworth. GL55 24 A2
Lower High St. GL55 24 B2
Neighbridge Ct. GL55 24 C1
Park Rd. GL55 24 A3
Pear Tree Clo. GL55 24 B3
Poplars Clo. GL55 24 A3
Rolling Stones. GL55 24 B2
Seymour Gate. GL55 24 B2
Sheep St. GL55 24 B2
Station Rd. GL55 24 C1
The Green. GL55 24 B3
The Leasows. GL55 24 A3
Westend Ter. GL55 24 B2
Wolds End Clo. GL55 24 B1

CINDERFORD

Abbey St. GL14 25 C2
Abbots Rd. GL14 25 D3
Albert Rd. GL14 25 B3
Albion Rd. GL14 25 C1
Ashdean. GL14 25 B1
Ashmead Rd. GL14 25 D3
Barleycorn Sq. GL14 25 B2
Beacons View Rd.
  GL14 25 D2
Beech Way. GL14 25 F2
Beechdean. GL14 25 B1
Belle Vue Rd. GL14 25 C2
Bilson. GL14 25 B1
Bilson Clo. GL14 25 B2
Birchwood Clo. GL14 25 A1
Broad St. GL14 25 E3
Brookside Rd. GL14 25 A1
Buckshaft Rd. GL14 25 C4
Cartway Grn. GL14 25 B2
Causeway Rd. GL14 25 C1
Church Rd. GL14 25 B4
Church St. GL14 25 F3
Church Walk. GL14 25 F3
College Rd. GL14 25 C2
Commercial St. GL14 25 C2
Coomb Dri. GL14 25 C4
Crabtree Rd. GL14 25 A1
Crawshay Pl. GL14 25 B2
Danby Clo. GL14 25 D2
Dean Cres. GL14 25 F3
Dockham Rd. GL14 25 C2
Double View. GL14 25 C3
Edge Hills Clo. GL14 25 C2
Edge Hills Rd. GL14 25 C2
Elmdean. GL14 25 B1
Elton Rd. GL14 25 F2
Fairfields. GL14 25 B2
Ferndale Rd. GL14 25 D1
Flaxley St. GL14 25 C3
Forest Rise. GL14 25 D1
Forest Rd. GL14 25 C2
Forest Vale Rd. GL14 25 A1
Foundry Rd. GL14 25 C2
Foxes Bridge Rd. GL14 25 B2
Furnaces Clo. GL14 25 B2
George La. GL14 25 E3
Greenhill Clo. GL14 25 D1
Greenway Rd. GL14 25 B4
Hastings Rd. GL14 25 B2
Hazeldean. GL14 25 B1
Heywood Rd. GL14 25 C2
High St,
  Cinderford. GL14 25 B1
High St,
  Littledean. GL14 25 E2
Highview Rd. GL14 25 D3
Hollydean. GL14 25 B1
Hollyhill Rd. GL14 25 A1
INDUSTRIAL & RETAIL:
Forest Vale
  Ind Est. GL14 25 A1
Station St
  Business Pk. GL14 25 B1
Kensley Vale. GL14 25 B3
Lamb La. GL14 25 C2

Lantern Clo. GL14 25 B2
Latimer Rd. GL14 25 D3
Laymore Rd. GL14 25 A1
Littledeanhill Rd. GL14 25 D3
Mapledean. GL14 25 B1
Market St. GL14 25 C2
Meadow Rd. GL14 25 D2
Meendhurst Rd. GL14 25 C3
Miners Walk. GL14 25 B2
Moorland Clo. GL14 25 D1
Mount Pleasant Rd.
  GL14 25 D3
Mountjoys La. GL14 25 C1
Mountjoys La End.
  GL14 25 C1
Mousel La. GL14 25 C3
Northwood Clo. GL14 25 C1
Oak Way. GL14 25 F2
Oakdean. GL14 25 B1
Oakwood Clo. GL14 25 D1
Office Rd. GL14 25 B3
Packers Rd. GL14 25 C2
Parragate. GL14 25 C1
Parragate Rd. GL14 25 B1
Pembroke St. GL14 25 D1
Pinewood Clo. GL14 25 C1
Prospect Rd. GL14 25 C2
Reddings La. GL14 25 D2
Roman Way. GL14 25 F2
Rowandean. GL14 25 C1
Ruspidge Rd. GL14 25 B4
St Annals Rd. GL14 25 D2
St Johns Sq. GL14 25 B4
St Whites Rd. GL14 25 B4
Seven Stars Rd. GL14 25 B1
Severn View. GL14 25 D2
Silver St. GL14 25 F3
Somerset Rd. GL14 25 B2
Southwood Clo. GL14 25 C1
Springfield Dri. GL14 25 C1
Station St. GL14 25 B2
Station Ter. GL14 25 B2
Stockwell Grn. GL14 25 C3
Sutton Rd. GL14 25 E3
The Buffit. GL14 25 E1
The Keelings. GL14 25 B2
The Oakfield. GL14 25 D2
Trinity Way. GL14 25 C1
Upper Bilson Rd. GL14 25 B1
Valley Rd. GL14 25 D3
Victoria Clo. GL14 25 B3
Victoria St. GL14 25 C2
Victoria Vale. GL14 25 C2
Wesley Rd. GL14 25 C3
West View. GL14 25 C3
Westerley Clo. GL14 25 C3
Westfield Ct. GL14 25 C1
Westfield Rd. GL14 25 C1
Willowdean. GL14 25 C1
Woodgate Rd. GL14 25 C1
Woodlands Rd. GL14 25 C3
Woodside Av. GL14 25 C3
Woodside St. GL14 25 C2
Woodside St. GL14 25 C2
Woodville Rd. GL14 25 D3
Worcester Rd. GL14 25 D2
York Rd. GL14 25 D2

CIRENCESTER

Abbey Way. GL7 26 B4
Abbots Rd. GL7 27 E5
Akeman Rd. GL7 27 E5
Albion St. GL7 26 B3
Alexander Dri. GL7 27 C7
Apsley Rd. GL7 27 B7
Apsley Rd. GL7 27 B7
Archery Rd. GL7 27 E5
Arnolds Way. GL7 26 E4
Ashcroft Gdns. GL7 27 C5
Ashcroft Rd. GL7 27 C5
Austin Rd. GL7 27 E5
Barn Way. GL7 26 A2
Barton La. GL7 26 B4
Bathurst Rd. GL7 27 B7
Baunton La. GL7 26 A1
Beaufort Ct. GL7 27 C7
Beech Gro. GL7 27 D5
Beeches Rd. GL7 27 D5
Berkeley Rd. GL7 27 C8
Berry Hill Cres. GL7 26 C3
Berry Hill Rd. GL7 26 C3
Bishops Walk. GL7 27 C5
Black Jack St. GL7 27 C5
Blake Rd. GL7 26 C4

Blue Quarry Rd. GL7 27 E5
Bluebell Dri. GL7 27 E8
Bowling Green Av.
  GL7 26 C3
Bowling Green La.
  GL7 26 B4
Bowling Green Rd.
  GL7 26 C3
Bowly Rd. GL7 27 D7
Bridge Clo. GL7 27 D7
Bridge End. GL7 27 D7
Bridge Rd. GL7 27 D7
Bristol Rd. GL7 27 B6
Brooke Rd. GL7 27 B7
Burford Rd. GL7 26 E4
Cambray Ct. GL7 27 D5
Carpenters La. GL7 27 D5
Castle St. GL7 27 C5
Cecily Hill. GL7 27 B5
Century Clo. GL7 27 F5
Cheltenham Rd. GL7 26 B3
Cherry Tree Dri. GL7 27 E7
Cherrytree La. GL7 26 F3
Chester Cres. GL7 27 D7
Chester St. GL7 27 D6
Chesterton Gro. GL7 27 C7
Chesterton La. GL7 27 A6
Chesterton Park. GL7 27 A6
Church Av. GL7 27 E8
Church St. GL7 27 D6
Churchill Rd. GL7 27 E5
City Bank Rd. GL7 27 D6
Coach House Mews.
  GL7 27 D5
College View. GL7 27 B8
Corinium Gate. GL7 27 D5
Cotswold Av. GL7 27 B5
Cotswold Clo. GL7 27 B6
Countess Lilias Rd.
  GL7 27 B7
Coxwell St. GL7 27 E5
Crabtree La. GL7 27 E6
Cranhams La. GL7 27 A7
Cricklade Rd. GL7 27 E7
Cricklade St. GL7 27 C5
Cripps Rd. GL7 27 C5
Dollar St. GL7 26 C4
Donside. GL7 26 A2
Drift Clo. GL7 27 A7
Drift Way. GL7 27 A7
Dugdale Rd. GL7 26 C4
Dyer St. GL7 26 C4
Edgeworth Clo. GL7 27 A7
Elliot Rd. GL7 27 E5
Elphick Rd. GL7 26 A2
Ermin Pl. GL7 27 E7
Esland Pl. GL7 27 D7
Estcote Rd. GL7 26 C4
Fairfax Clo. GL7 27 C7
Fairfax Rd. GL7 27 C7
Farrell Clo. GL7 27 C5
Fosse Clo. GL7 26 E4
Foxes Bank Dri. GL7 27 B7
Foxglove Clo. GL7 27 C7
Gallows Pound La. GL7 26 B2
Garden Clo. GL7 27 C6
Gardner St. GL7 27 D6
*Garland Ct,
  Meadow Rd. GL7 27 C7
Gibson Ct. GL7 27 C7
Glebe Clo. GL7 26 B2
Gloucester Rd. GL7 26 A1
Gloucester St. GL7 26 B4
Golden Farm Rd. GL7 26 B4
Gooseacre Ct. GL7 26 B4
Gooseacre La. GL7 26 B4
Gosditch St. GL7 27 C5
Grange Ct. GL7 26 B1
Grantley Cres. GL7 27 C7
Greyfriars Walk. GL7 27 B8
Grove La. GL7 26 C4
Hakeburn Rd. GL7 26 C4
Hammond Way. GL7 27 B8
Hanover Ct. GL7 27 D6
Hanstone Clo. GL7 27 B7
Haresfield. GL7 26 B1
Haygarth Clo. GL7 27 B7
Herbert Stalk Clo. GL7 27 E5
Hereward Rd. GL7 26 C4
INDUSTRIAL & RETAIL:
Love La Ind Est. GL7 27 D7
The Corinium
  Centre. GL7 27 D8
Jobbins Ct. GL7 27 C5
Kemble Dri. GL7 27 A7
King St. GL7 27 D6
Kings Way. GL7 27 F7

Belgrave Rd. GL1 30 D3
Belgrove Ter. GL1 31 E4
Berkeley St. GL1 30 D2
Bibury Rd. GL4 31 E5
Billingham Clo. GL4 31 G5
Birch Av. GL4 31 G5
Birchmore Rd. GL1 31 F3
Bishopstone Rd. GL1 31 F3
Bittern Av. GL4 31 H5
Blackfriars. GL1 30 D2
Blenheim Rd. GL1 31 E3
Blinkhorns Bridge La. GL2 31 G2
Bloomfield Rd. GL1 30 C5
Bloomfield Ter. GL1 30 C5
Bowly Rd. GL1 30 C6
Bradford Rd. GL2 31 G1
Braeburn Clo. GL2 31 H1
Bridge Clo. GL2 30 A5
Bristol Rd. GL2 30 B6
Broadway. GL4 31 E6
Brook St. GL1 30 D4
Brookside Villas. GL2 31 G2
Brunswick Rd. GL1 30 D3
Brunswick Sq. GL1 30 D3
Bruton Way. GL1 31 E1
Bull La. GL1 30 D2
Bullfinch Rd. GL4 31 H5
Burford Mews. GL1 31 F3
Caesar Rd. GL2 30 B6
Cambridge St. GL1 31 E2
Carlton Rd. GL1 30 D6
Carmarthen St. GL1 31 E4
Carne Pl. GL4 31 H2
Casey Clo. GL1 31 F2
Cecil Rd. GL1 30 C5
Cemetery Rd. GL4 31 F5
Central Rd. GL1 30 D4
Chancel Clo. GL4 31 G3
Charles St. GL1 31 E3
Chartwell Clo. GL2 30 A5
Chase La. GL4 31 G4
Cheltenham Rd. GL2 31 F1
Chequers Rd. GL4 31 F4
Chester Rd. GL4 31 H3
Cheyney Clo. GL4 31 G5
Church St. GL1 30 C3
Church Way. GL4 31 H5
Churchill Rd. GL1 30 C4
Clare St. GL1 30 C1
Claremont Rd. GL1 31 E1
Clarence St. GL1 30 D2
Clegram Rd. GL1 30 C4
Clement St. GL1 31 F4
Clevedon Rd. GL1 31 E5
Clifton Rd. GL1 30 C4
Coldray Clo. GL1 31 F2
Colin Rd. GL4 31 H2
Colingbourne Rd. GL4 31 F5
College Ct. GL1 30 D1
College St. GL1 30 D1
Coltman Clo. GL1 31 G2
Columbia Clo. GL1 31 E1
Commercial Rd. GL1 30 C2
Concorde Way. GL4 31 G5
Conduit St. GL1 31 E4
Coney Hill Par. GL4 31 H5
Coney Hill Rd. GL4 31 G4
Coronation Gro. GL2 31 G2
Cotteswold Rd. GL4 31 F6
County Cres. GL1 31 E2
Court Gdns. GL2 30 A5
Court Pl. GL4 31 H5
Cromwell St. GL1 30 D3
Crosskeys La. GL1 30 D2
Curlew Rd. GL4 31 H6
Dainty St. GL1 31 E4
Deans Walk. GL1 30 D1
Denmark Rd. GL1 31 F1
Derby Ct. GL1 31 F3
Derby Rd. GL1 31 F3
Dickens Clo. GL4 31 E6
Dinely St. GL1 31 E3
Dorney Rd. GL1 30 D5
Dorritt Clo. GL1 31 E5
Ducie St. GL1 31 E4
Durham Rd. GL4 31 H3
Dynevor St. GL1 31 E4
Eagle Way. GL4 31 H6
Eastbrook Rd. GL4 31 H3
Eastern Av. GL4 31 G5
Eastgate St. GL1 30 D2
Eastville Clo. GL4 31 G4
Ebor Rd. GL2 31 G2
Elmbridge Rd. GL2 31 H2
Empire Way. GL2 30 B6
Estcourt Rd. GL1 31 G1
Etheridge Pl. GL1 31 F2
Fairford Way. GL4 31 G5
Falkner St. GL1 31 E3
Faraday Clo. GL1 31 E5
Farm Mews. GL1 30 D4
Farm St. GL1 30 D4
Fieldfare. GL4 31 H6
Filton Way. GL4 31 G5
Finlay Pl. GL4 31 E6
Finlay Rd. GL4 31 E6
Forsyte Way. GL4 31 G5
Frampton Rd. GL1 30 C4
Furlong Rd. GL1 30 D4
Garlandstone Wk. GL2 30 B5
Gladstone Rd. GL1 30 C5
Goldsborough Clo. GL4 31 G5
Goodwin Ct. GL1 30 D5
Goodyere St. GL1 31 E3
Gothic Cott. GL1 31 E3
Gouda Way. GL1 30 D1
Grafton Rd. GL2 31 G1
Granville St. GL1 30 C5
Great Western Rd. GL1 31 E1
Green Pippin Clo. GL2 31 H2
Greyfriars. GL1 30 D2
Grosvenor Rd. GL2 31 G1
Grove Cres. GL4 31 H2
Grove St. GL1 31 E4
Hailes Rd. GL4 31 H4
Hamer St. GL1 31 F2
Hampden Way. GL1 30 D2
Hanman Rd. GL1 31 E4
Harbury Mews. GL1 31 F3
Hare La. GL1 30 D1
Harness Clo. GL1 30 B5
Hartington Rd. GL1 30 C5
Hartland Rd. GL1 31 E6
Hatfield Rd. GL1 31 F4
Hatherley Rd. GL1 31 E5
Haven Ct. GL2 31 H1
Hawk Clo. GL4 31 H6
Hawthorne Av. GL4 31 H6
Hazelton Clo. GL4 31 E6
Heathville Rd. GL1 31 E1
Hemmingsdale Rd. GL2 30 B3
Hempstead By-Pass. GL2 30 B6
Hempsted La. GL2 30 A5
Henley Pl. GL1 30 D6
Henry Rd. GL1 31 E1
Henry St. GL1 31 E1
Herbert St. GL1 31 F3
Heron Way. GL4 31 H6
Hethersett Rd. GL1 31 F3
High Orchard St. GL1 30 C3
High St. GL1 31 E4
High View. GL2 30 A5
Highfield Rd. GL4 31 G5
Highworth Rd. GL1 31 E5
Hillfield Court Rd. GL1 31 F1
Hilton Clo. GL2 30 A5
Honeythorne Clo. GL2 30 A4
Honyatt Rd. GL1 31 E1
Hooper Clo. GL4 31 G5
Hopewell St. GL1 31 E3
Horseshoe Way. GL2 30 B5
Horton Rd. GL1 31 F2
Howard St. GL1 30 D4
Huxley Rd. GL1 31 E5
Hyde Clo. GL1 31 F1
Hyde La. GL1 31 E1
India Rd. GL1 31 F3
INDUSTRIAL & RETAIL:
Ashville Ind Est. GL2 30 B6
Morelands Trading Est. GL1 30 C4
Jersey Rd. GL1 31 E3
Kaskelot Way. GL2 30 B5
Kencourt Clo. GL2 31 G1
Kenilworth Av. GL2 31 F1
Kimbrose Way. GL1 30 C3
King Edwards Av. GL1 30 D5
Kings Barton St. GL1 31 E2
Kings Walk. GL1 30 D2
Kingsley Rd. GL4 31 F6
Kitchener Av. GL1 30 D6
Knowles Rd. GL1 31 E4
Laburnum Rd. GL1 30 C6
Ladybellegate St. GL1 30 C2
Ladysmith Rd. GL1 30 D6
Ladywell Clo. GL2 30 A5
Lannett Rd. GL1 30 D5
Larkspear Clo. GL1 30 D6
Leonard Rd. GL1 31 E5
Lewisham Rd. GL1 30 D6
Lichfield Rd. GL4 31 H3
Lime Tree Ct. GL1 30 D6
Linden Rd. GL1 30 C5
Linnet Clo. GL4 31 G6
Llandilo St. GL1 31 E4
Llanthony Rd. GL1 30 C2
London Rd. GL1 31 E1
Longsmith St. GL1 30 D2
Lonsdale Rd. GL2 31 H1
Lower Quay St. GL1 30 C1
Lysons Av. GL1 30 C5
Madleaze Rd. GL1 30 C4
Magdala Rd. GL1 31 E3
Malmesbury Rd. GL4 31 F4
Mansell Clo. GL2 30 B6
Market Par. GL1 30 D2
Marlborough Cres. GL4 31 F5
Marlborough Rd. GL4 31 F5
Massey Pde. GL1 31 E5
Massey Rd. GL1 31 F5
Matson Pl. GL1 31 F5
Mayfair Clo. GL2 30 B4
Maytree Sq. GL4 31 H5
Melbourne St E. GL1 31 E4
Melbourne St W. GL1 31 E4
Merchants Rd. GL1 30 C3
Merevale Rd. GL2 31 G1
Metz Way. GL1 31 E2
Midland Rd. GL1 30 D4
Midsummer Walk. GL2 30 B5
Mill St. GL1 31 F3
Millbrook Clo. GL1 31 F3
Millbrook St. GL1 31 E3
Milo Pl. GL1 30 D5
Montpellier. GL1 30 D3
Montpellier Mews. GL1 30 D3
Moor St. GL1 31 E4
Morelands Gro. GL1 31 E6
Morpeth St. GL1 31 E4
Morton St. GL1 31 E4
Morton Cotts. GL1 31 E3
Mount St. GL1 30 C1
Myers Rd. GL1 31 F2
Napier St. GL1 31 E2
Naunton Rd. GL4 31 H4
Nelson St. GL1 31 E5
Nettleton Rd. GL1 31 E2
New Inn La. GL1 30 D2
New St. GL1 30 D4
Newark Rd. GL1 30 B5
Newland St. GL1 31 E1
Newton Av. GL4 31 G5
Norbury Av. GL4 31 G6
Norfolk St. GL1 30 C3
Norman Ball Way. GL1 31 F2
Northbrook Rd. GL4 31 H2
Northfield Rd. GL4 31 E6
Northfield Sq. GL4 31 E6
Northgate St. GL1 30 D2
Nut Croft. GL4 31 G4
Old Painswick Rd. GL4 31 G5
Old Row. GL1 31 E3
Old Tram Rd. GL1 30 D3
Oriole Way. GL4 31 H5
Osric Rd. GL1 31 E5
Overbrook Clo. GL4 31 H3
Overbury Rd. GL1 31 F3
Oxford Rd. GL1 31 E1
Oxford St. GL1 31 E1
Oxford Ter. GL1 31 E1
Painswick Rd. GL4 31 G5
Park Rd. GL1 30 D3
Park St. GL1 30 D1
Parkend Rd. GL1 30 D4
Parliament St. GL1 30 D2
Parry Rd. GL1 31 E5
Paul St. GL1 31 E4
Peart Clo. GL1 31 F2
Pembroke St. GL1 31 E3
Percy St. GL1 31 E4
Philip St. GL1 30 C4
Pineway. GL4 31 G6
Pitt St. GL1 30 D1
Podsmead Pl. GL1 30 C6
Podsmead Rd. GL1 30 C6
Price St. GL1 30 C4
Prince St. GL1 31 E2
Quay St. GL1 30 C1
Raglan St. GL1 31 E3
Raikes Rd. GL1 30 C5
Ravis Clo. GL4 31 G5
Rea La. GL2 30 A5
Rectory La. GL2 30 A5
Red Lion Ct. GL1 31 F3
Red Poll Way. GL4 31 H6
Redstart Way. GL4 31 H5
Regent St. GL1 31 E4
Reservoir Rd. GL4 31 F6
Richmond Av. GL4 31 G5
Riversley Rd. GL2 31 G1
Robinhood St. GL1 30 C4
Robinson Rd. GL1 30 D4
Rosebery Av. GL1 30 D6
Royal La. GL1 31 E1
Russell St. GL1 31 E2
Ryecroft St. GL1 31 E3
Saffron Clo. GL4 31 F6
St Albans Rd. GL2 30 B6
St Aldate St. GL1 30 D2
St Aldwyn Rd. GL1 31 E5
St Ann Way. GL1 30 C3
St Catherine Ct. GL1 30 D4
St Catherine St. GL1 30 D1
St James St. GL1 31 E4
St Johns La. GL1 30 D2
St Lukes St. GL1 30 C2
St Marys Sq. GL1 30 D1
St Marys St. GL1 30 D1
St Michaels Sq. GL1 30 D2
St Oswalds Rd. GL1 30 C1
St Pauls Ct. GL1 30 D4
St Pauls Rd. GL1 30 D4
St Swithuns Rd. GL2 30 A5
Saintbridge Clo. GL4 31 G6
Saintbridge Pl. GL4 31 G6
Salisbury Rd. GL1 31 F4
Sandalwood Dri. GL2 30 B4
Sandyleaze. GL2 31 H1
Sapperton Rd. GL4 31 E6
Savernake Rd. GL4 31 F4
Selwyn Rd. GL4 31 E6
Severn Rd. GL1 30 C2
Seymour Rd. GL1 30 C5
Sherborne St. GL1 31 E1
Sidney St. GL1 31 F3
Sinope St. GL1 31 E3
Sisson End. GL2 31 H1
Sisson Rd. GL2 31 H1
Skinner St. GL1 30 D1
Skylark Way. GL4 31 G6
Slaney St. GL1 31 E4
Somerset Pl. GL1 30 C3
Soren Larsen Way. GL2 30 B5
Southbrook Rd. GL4 31 H3
Southfield Rd. GL4 31 E6
Southgate St. GL1 30 C3
Spa Rd. GL1 30 C3
Spinnaker Rd. GL2 30 B3
Stanley Rd. GL1 30 D5
Stanley Ter. GL1 30 D5
Stanway Rd. GL4 31 H4
Station Rd. GL1 31 E2
Stirrup Clo. GL2 30 B5
Stonechat Av. GL4 31 H6
Stonehenge Rd. GL4 31 F4
Stow Clo. GL4 31 E6
Stratton Rd. GL1 31 E3
Stroud Rd. GL1 30 C3
Sudbrook Way. GL4 31 G6
Sudmeadow Rd. GL2 30 B2
Sweetbriar St. GL1 31 E1
Swift Rd. GL4 31 H6
Sybil Rd. GL1 31 E5
Sydenham Ter. GL1 30 D5
Talbot Mews. GL1 30 A6
Tarrington Rd. GL1 31 E5
Teddington Gdns. GL4 31 G6
Tern Clo. GL4 31 H5
The Anchorage. GL2 30 B6
The Chestnuts. GL1 30 C3
The Conifers. GL1 31 F4
The Firs. GL1 31 E1
The Gallops. GL2 30 B5
The Lampreys. GL4 31 G5
The Laurels. GL1 31 E4
The Oval. GL1 30 C6
The Oxebode. GL1 30 D2
The Paddock. GL2 30 A5
The Quay. GL1 30 C1
Theresa St. GL1 30 C4
Thomas St. GL1 31 E3
Thornhill Clo. GL1 30 C6
Thrush Clo. GL4 31 H5
Tredworth Rd. GL1 31 E4
Trier Way. GL1 30 C3
Tudor St. GL1 30 C5
Tuffley Av. GL1 30 B5
Tuffley Cres. GL1 30 C6
Tweenbrook Av. GL1 30 D5
Ullenwood Rd. GL4 31 H4
Union St. GL1 31 E1
Upper Quay St. GL1 30 C1
Upton St. GL1 31 F4
Vauxhall Rd. GL1 31 E3
Vauxhall Ter. GL1 31 E3
Vicarage Rd. GL1 31 F4
Victoria St. GL1 31 E3
Victory Rd. GL1 31 E5
Waters Reach. GL2 30 A5
Waverley Rd. GL2 31 G1
Wellesley St. GL1 31 E5
Wellington St. GL1 31 D3
Wells Rd. GL4 31 H3
Wesley Ct. GL1 31 E3
Westgate St. GL1 30 C2
Weston Rd. GL1 30 D3
Wheatstone Rd. GL1 31 E5
Widden St. GL1 31 E3
Willow Av. GL4 31 G4
Willow Way. GL4 31 G5
Wilton Clo. GL1 30 C5
Wilton Rd. GL1 30 C6
Windfall Way. GL2 31 H1
Windmill Cotts. GL1 31 F3
Wolseley Rd. GL2 31 G1
Woodcock Clo. GL4 31 H6
Woodford Clo. GL4 31 F5
Worcester St. GL1 30 D1
Wotton Hill. GL2 31 F1
Wren Clo. GL4 31 G6
York Rd. GL4 31 H3

KINGSWOOD

Abbots Av. BS15 32 A6
Abbots Wood. BS15 32 A4
Albert Rd. BS15 32 A6
Aldermoor Way. BS30 32 B6
Alexandra Rd. BS15 32 A5
Alfred Lovell Gdns. BS30 32 D6
Allington Dri. BS30 32 C6
Alma Clo. BS15 32 B2
Alma Rd. BS15 32 B2
Alsop Rd. BS15 32 A2
Alwins Ct. BS30 32 C6
Amble Clo. BS15 32 C3
Anchor Rd. BS15 32 D1
Ashford Way. BS15 32 D4
Ashley. BS15 32 C3
Avon Ring Rd. BS30 32 C5
Baden Rd. BS15 32 D3
Bank Rd. BS15 32 B2
Barn Wood Clo. BS15 32 C2
Barrington Clo. BS15 32 C1
Barrington Ct. BS15 32 C1
Barrs Court Av. BS30 32 D5
Barrs Court Rd. BS30 32 D5
Barrs Ct. BS30 32 C6
Baxter Clo. BS15 32 C3
Beaconlea. BS15 32 A4
Beech Clo. BS30 32 D5
Beechwood Av. BS15 32 A5
Bellevue Clo. BS15 32 C3
Bellevue Rd. BS15 32 C3
Belsher Dri. BS15 32 D4
Berkeley Rd. BS15 32 B3
Betjeman Ct. BS30 32 D6
Bibstone. BS15 32 D2
Bickford Clo. BS30 32 D5
Birdwood. BS15 32 A5
Birkdale. BS30 32 D4
Blackhorse Rd. BS15 32 A3
Blackthorn Walk. BS15 32 B1
Bodey Clo. BS30 32 D5
Boultons La Rd. BS15 32 A2
Brake Clo. BS15 32 C4
Bramley Ct. BS30 32 C6
Bredon Clo. BS15 32 C4
Bright St. BS15 32 A3
Brighton Pl. BS15 32 A2
Britannia Rd. BS15 32 A3
Brompton Clo. BS15 32 C3
Brook Rd. BS15 32 D2
Burnham Clo. BS15 32 C2
Burnham Dri. BS15 32 C2
Cadbury Heath Rd. BS30 32 D5
Caddick Clo. BS15 32 C1
Cade Clo. BS15 32 C4
Cains Clo. BS15 32 B4
Castle Rd. BS15 32 A1
Causley Dri. BS30 32 C6
Cecil Rd. BS15 32 A3
Cennick Av. BS15 32 B2
Central Av. BS15 32 A6
Champion Rd. BS15 32 C1
Charfield. BS15 32 D3
Chase Rd. BS15 32 A1

Chavenage. BS15 32 D2
Chesham Way. BS15 32 A1
Chipperfield Dri. BS15 32 C2
Chubb Clo. BS30 32 C5
Church Rd. BS15 32 B2
Churchill Clo. BS30 32 D6
Clare Rd. BS15 32 A1
Claypool Rd. BS15 32 B4
Coberley. BS15 32 A4
Cock Rd. BS15 32 B5
Collingwood Av. BS15 32 B2
Colthurst Dri. BS15 32 B6
Copley Ct. BS15 32 B6
Coronation Clo. BS30 32 D6
Coronation Rd. BS15 32 C3
Coronation Rd. BS30 32 D6
Cotswold View. BS15 32 A1
Cottington Ct. BS15 32 B6
Counterpool Rd. BS15 32 A3
Court Rd. BS15 32 B5
Courtney Clo. BS15 32 C4
Courtney Rd. BS15 32 B3
Courtney Way. BS15 32 C3
Cox Ct. BS30 32 C6
Cradock Clo. BS30 32 D6
Cranham Clo. BS15 32 C1
Crates Clo. BS15 32 C2
Craven Way. BS30 32 C1
Crispin Way. BS15 32 C1
Cromwell Ct. BS15 32 B6
Cross St. BS15 32 A2
Crown Hill. BS15 32 A1
Crown Rd. BS15 32 A1
Danesbury. BS15 32 B6
Davis Clo. BS30 32 C6
Dawn Rise. BS15 32 C2
Deanery Rd. BS15 32 D3
Derrick Rd. BS15 32 A3
Deverose Ct. BS15 32 B6
Dorset Rd. BS15 32 A2
Douglas Rd. BS15 32 A4
Downend Rd. BS15 32 A1
Downside Clo. BS30 32 C5
Dudley Ct. BS30 32 C6
Dundry Clo. BS15 32 B4
Dylan Thomas Ct.
  BS30 32 D6
Dyrham Clo. BS15 32 C2
Dyrham Rd. BS15 32 C2
Earlstone Clo. BS30 32 D6
Earlstone Cres. BS30 32 D6
Edgecombe Clo. BS15 32 C2
Edward Rd. BS15 32 B3
Elberton. BS15 32 D3
Ellesmere Rd. BS15 32 A3
Elm Rd. BS15 32 B4
Elm Tree Clo. BS15 32 A2
Elm Tree Way. BS15 32 B2
Elmfield. BS15 32 B4
Elmfield Clo. BS15 32 B4
Fairford Clo. BS15 32 C1
Fairview Rd. BS15 32 C3
Filwood Dri. BS15 32 C2
Fisher Av. BS15 32 D1
Fisher Rd. BS15 32 D1
Footshill Rd. BS15 32 A4
Forde Clo. BS30 32 C5
Forest Edge. BS15 32 A6
Forest Rd. BS15 32 A4
Forest Walk. BS15 32 A3
Fountains Dri. BS30 32 C5
Foxcote. BS15 32 C3
Frys Hill. BS15 32 B1
Furzewood Rd. BS15 32 C3
Gages Clo. BS15 32 C3
Gages Rd. BS15 32 C4
Gee Moors. BS15 32 C4
Gilbert Rd. BS15 32 A2
Gilpin Clo. BS15 32 C1
Gingell Clo. BS15 32 C4
Gladstone Rd. BS15 32 A1
Glanville Gdns. BS15 32 B4
Glastonbury Clo. BS30 32 C5
Grace Dri. BS15 32 D2
Grange Av. BS15 32 A6
Grannys La. BS15 32 B5
Grantham La. BS15 32 A2
Grantham Rd. BS15 32 A2
Greenbank Rd. BS15 32 A5
Greenore. BS15 32 A4
Greenways. BS15 32 D2
Gregory Ct. BS30 32 D5
Greve Ct. BS30 32 C6
Grimsbury Rd. BS15 32 D3
Gunning Clo. BS15 32 C4
Hale Clo. BS15 32 B6
Halls Rd. BS15 32 A3

Hampton Clo. BS30 32 D6
Hampton St. BS15 32 A1
Hanbury Clo. BS15 32 A6
Hanham Mount. BS15 32 A5
Hanham Rd. BS15 32 A4
Hardy Ct. BS30 32 C6
Harptree Ct. BS30 32 D6
Haskins Ct. BS30 32 D6
Headington Clo. BS15 32 A6
Henry Wiliamson Ct.
  BS30 32 D6
Hickling Ct. BS15 32 B2
High Elm. BS15 32 B4
High St,
  Kingswood. BS15 32 B2
Highfield Av. BS15 32 A6
Highview Rd. BS15 32 C1
Hill St. BS15 32 C3
Hollow Rd. BS15 32 B2
Holly Cres. BS15 32 C2
Holly Grn. BS15 32 D1
Holly Hill Rd. BS15 32 C2
Hollyguest Rd. BS15 32 A5
Holmwood. BS15 32 A5
Home Mead. BS30 32 D6
Honey Hill Rd. BS15 32 C2
Honey Way. BS15 32 C2
Hopps Rd. BS15 32 A3
Horsecroft Gdns. BS30 32 D5
Horwood Ct. BS30 32 D6
Howes Clo. BS30 32 D5
Hunters Dri. BS15 32 C2
Iles Clo. BS15 32 A6

INDUSTRIAL & RETAIL:
Kingswood Trading
  Est. BS15 32 A2
Ingleside Rd. BS15 32 A1
Johnson Dri. BS30 32 C5
Kelston Gro. BS15 32 B5
Kemble Clo. BS15 32 B4
Kennington Av. BS15 32 A2
Kennmoor Clo. BS30 32 D5
Kensit Clo. BS15 32 C4
Kents Grn. BS15 32 B1
Kimberley Rd. BS15 32 A2
Kingsfield La. BS15 32 B5
Kingsholme Rd. BS15 32 A1
Kingsleigh Ct. BS15 32 C3
Kingsleigh Gdns. BS15 32 C3
Kingsleigh Park. BS15 32 C3
Kyght Clo. BS15 32 C3
Lacock Dri. BS30 32 C5
Ladd Clo. BS15 32 C4
Langford Way. BS15 32 B4
Lansdown View. BS15 32 B4
Laurel St. BS15 32 A3
Laurie Lee Ct. BS30 32 D6
Lavers Clo. BS15 32 B4
Lees Hill. BS15 32 B1
Lintern Cres. BS30 32 D5
Lintham Dri. BS15 32 C4
London St. BS15 32 A2
Loughman Clo. BS15 32 B2
Lower Cock Rd. BS15 32 C4
Lower Hanham Rd.
  BS15 32 A5
Lynton. BS15 32 D2
Macdonald Wk. BS15 32 A2
Maesbury. BS15 32 B5
Malmesbury Clo. BS30 32 C5
Maple Ct. BS15 32 A2
Marsham Way. BS30 32 C6
May St. BS15 32 A1
Miles Ct. BS30 32 C6
Milner Grn. BS30 32 D5
Moravian Rd. BS15 32 A2
Morley Ter. BS15 32 A1
Mount Gdns. BS15 32 A4
Mount Hill Rd. BS15 32 A4
Muirfield. BS30 32 D4
Mulberry Clo. BS15 32 C2
Mulberry Rd. BS15 32 C2
Neville Rd. BS15 32 B1
New Cheltenham Rd.
  BS15 32 B1
Newton Clo. BS15 32 D2
Newton Dri. BS30 32 D6
Newton Rd. BS30 32 D6
Niblett Clo. BS15 32 B1
North Park. BS15 32 B1
Northend Av. BS15 32 B1
Northend Gdns. BS15 32 B1
Northend Rd. BS15 32 B1
Northfield Av. BS15 32 A6
Norton Clo. BS15 32 C3

Nymps Field. BS15 32 B1
Oakfield Rd. BS15 32 A4
Oakridge Clo. BS15 32 D3
Oram Ct. BS30 32 D6
Orchard Clo. BS15 32 B3
Orchard Gdns. BS15 32 C3
Orchard Rd. BS15 32 B3
Orchard Vale. BS15 32 C3
Owls Head Rd. BS15 32 A5
Ozleworth. BS15 32 D3
Palmers Clo. BS30 32 D5
Park Clo. BS15 32 B3
Park Rd. BS15 32 B2
Park View. BS15 32 B3
Parklands. BS15 32 C3
Parkwall Rd. BS30 32 D6
Parkwell Cres. BS30 32 D6
Peacocks La. BS15 32 A3
Penard Way. BS15 32 C3
Perrot Rd. BS15 32 D2
Petherton Clo. BS15 32 B3
Pettigrove Gdns. BS15 32 B4
Pettigrove Rd. BS15 32 B4
Pillingers Rd. BS15 32 A2
Pine Wood. BS15 32 C1
Pippin Ct. BS30 32 C6
Poplar Ter. BS15 32 C6
Pound Rd. BS15 32 A5
Pows Rd. BS15 32 A3
Press Moor Dri. BS30 32 C6
Purton Clo. BS15 32 B4
Quarry Rd. BS15 32 A5
Quarter Mile Alley.
  BS15 32 B1
Queens Rd. BS30 32 D6
Regent St. BS15 32 A2
Rodborough Way.
  BS15 32 D4
Runnymede. BS15 32 B2
Russell Av. BS15 32 B4
Russell Ct. BS15 32 C3
St Andrews. BS30 32 D4
St Davids Av. BS15 32 D5
Sassoon Ct. BS30 32 D6
School Rd. BS15 32 A3
School Rd. BS30 32 D6
Scott Ct. BS30 32 C6
Selkirk Rd. BS15 32 A1
Selworthy. BS15 32 B3
Seymour Rd. BS15 32 A2
Sherbourne Clo. BS15 32 C1
Shilton Clo. BS15 32 C3
Shortwood View. BS15 32 C2
Siston Common. BS15 32 D1
Skippon Ct. BS15 32 B6
Somerton Clo. BS15 32 B4
Soundwell Rd. BS15 32 B4
South Rd. BS15 32 A3
Southall Av. BS15 32 B2
Southey Av. BS15 32 B2
Spring Hill. BS15 32 B1
Stafford Clo. BS30 32 D5
Stanton Clo. BS15 32 B1
Staverton Way. BS15 32 D4
Staynes Cres. BS30 32 C6
Stephens Dri. BS30 32 C6
Stokes Ct. BS30 32 C6
Stone Hill. BS15 32 B6
Stoneleigh Dri. BS30 32 C6
Stourton Dri. BS30 32 C6
Swaish Dri. BS30 32 C6
Syston Way. BS15 32 A1
Tanner Clo. BS30 32 C5
Taylor Clo. BS15 32 C2
Tennis Court Rd. BS15 32 D1
The Haven. BS15 32 B1
The Meadows. BS15 32 A6
The Orchards. BS15 32 C3
The Park. BS15 32 B2
The Ride. BS15 32 D1
The Twynings. BS15 32 B1
Tibberton. BS15 32 D2
Tintern Clo. BS30 32 C5
Tippetts Rd. BS15 32 A1
Tower Rd. BS15 32 A1
Trevethin Clo. BS15 32 C6
Troon Rd. BS15 32 D4
Turnberry. BS30 32 D4
Tyler Clo. BS15 32 B5
Tyndale Rd. BS15 32 B1
Unity St. BS15 32 A1
Victoria Park. BS15 32 A2
Victoria Rd. BS15 32 C4
Walnut Clo. BS15 32 C2
Walnut Cres. BS15 32 D3
Walnut La. BS15 32 C4
Warner Clo. BS15 32 C4

Waters Rd. BS15 32 A2
Webb Clo. BS15 32 C4
Wedmore Clo. BS15 32 C4
Wellington Rd. BS15 32 A1
Wentworth. BS30 32 D4
Wesley Av. BS15 32 A5
Wesley Hill. BS15 32 A1
West St. BS15 32 A3
Westfield Clo. BS15 32 B6
Westons Way. BS15 32 C4
Whitecroft Way. BS15 32 D4
Whitefield Clo. BS15 32 A5
Whittucks Clo. BS15 32 A6
Whittucks Rd. BS15 32 A6
Willis Rd. BS15 32 D1
Wilmot Ct. BS30 32 D5
Wilshire Av. BS15 32 A5
Witcombe Clo. BS15 32 C1
Woburn Clo. BS15 32 C5
Wood Rd. BS15 32 A3
Woodcote. BS15 32 A5
Woodend. BS15 32 A4
Woodington Ct. BS30 32 C6
Woodland Ter. BS15 32 B3
Woodstock. BS15 32 C3
Woodstock Clo. BS15 32 C3
Woodstock Rd. BS15 32 C3
Woody Leaze. BS15 32 A5
Woodyleaze Dri. BS15 32 A5
Worcester Rd. BS15 32 A2
Worthy Clo. BS15 32 C4
Wraxall Rd. BS30 32 D4
Wychwood. BS15 32 B4
Wyns Ct. BS15 32 B6

LECHLADE

Abbots Walk. GL7 33 C2
Bell La. GL7 33 B3
Briary Rd. GL7 33 C1
Bridge Walk. GL7 33 C3
Burford St. GL7 33 C2
Butlers Flat. GL7 33 B1
Chancel Way. GL7 33 C2
Cuthwine Pl. GL7 33 B2
East Allcourt. GL7 33 B2
Gassons Rd. GL7 33 B2
Gassons Way. GL7 33 B2
Hambidge La. GL7 33 B1
High St. GL7 33 B2
Katherines Walk. GL7 33 C2
Keble Clo. GL7 33 C1
Kingsmead. GL7 33 B1
Loders Field. GL7 33 C2
Market Pl. GL7 33 C3
Mill La. GL7 33 C2
Moorgate. GL7 33 A2
Oak St. GL7 33 C2
Orchard Clo. GL7 33 B3
Pigeon Clo. GL7 33 C1
Roman Way. GL7 33 C1
St Birinus Ct. GL7 33 B2
St Johns St. GL7 33 C3
St Lawrence Rd. GL7 33 C2
Shelleys Walk. GL7 33 C3
Sherborne St. GL7 33 B3
Station Rd. GL7 33 C1
Thames St. GL7 33 B3
The Cursus. GL7 33 B2
The Loders. GL7 33 B2
The Spinney. GL7 33 B3
West Allcourt. GL7 33 B3
West Way. GL7 33 C1
Wharf La. GL7 33 C3

LEONARD STANLEY/ KINGS STANLEY

Bath Rd. GL10 33 A5
Bathleaze. GL10 33 C4
Beeches Clo. GL10 33 C4
Borough Clo. GL10 33 C6
Brimley. GL10 33 B5
Broad St. GL10 33 C5
Brockley Rd. GL10 33 B4
Castle Mead. GL10 33 C4
Castle St. GL10 33 B6
Church Rd. GL10 33 A5
Church St. GL10 33 C5
Coldwell. GL10 33 D6
Coldwell Clo. GL10 33 D6
Coldwell Rd. GL10 33 D6
Coombe La. GL10 33 D6

Daffodil Leaze. GL10 33 D6
Dozule Clo. GL10 33 B5
Elm Clo. GL10 33 C4
Elmlea Rd. GL10 33 C4
Gardeners Way. GL10 33 C5
Guildings Way. GL10 33 C4
Gypsy La. GL10 33 A6
High St. GL10 33 C5
Mankley Rd. GL10 33 B5
Marsh La. GL10 33 B6
Marsh Mews. GL10 33 B5
Marsh Rd. GL10 33 B5
New St. GL10 33 C5
Orchard Clo. GL10 33 D6
Penn La. GL10 33 D6
St Georges Av. GL10 33 C4
St Georges Clo. GL10 33 B4
Selwyn Clo. GL10 33 C4
Shute St. GL10 33 C5
Tannery Clo. GL10 33 A5
Tannery Cotts. GL10 33 A5
The Luggs. GL10 33 C5
The Nursery. GL10 33 C5
The Street. GL10 33 A5
Wesley Ct. GL10 33 A5
Woodlands. GL10 33 A5
Woodside La. GL10 33 B6

LYDNEY

Albert St. GL15 34 B2
Almond Walk. GL15 34 B2
Ash Clo. GL15 34 B2
Augustus Way. GL15 34 C1
Avenue Andre Clement.
  GL15 34 B4
Bath Pl. GL15 34 B3
Bathurst Park Rd. GL15 34 B3
Beauchamp Mdw.
  GL15 34 C2
Beaufort Dri. GL15 34 C4
Berkeley Cres. GL15 34 B1
Bishops Gate. GL15 34 A4
Bracken Clo. GL15 34 C3
Bracken Dri. GL15 34 C3
Bream Rd. GL15 34 A2
Caesars Clo. GL15 34 C2
Cambourne Pl. GL15 34 C4
Centurion Rd. GL15 34 C2
Chantry Clo. GL15 34 A5
Charnwood Clo. GL15 34 B1
Cherry Walk. GL15 34 B2
Church Gdns. GL15 34 B4
Church Rd. GL15 34 A4
Claudius Way. GL15 34 C2
Cookson Ter. GL15 34 B6
Crump Pl. GL15 34 D4
Darters Clo. GL15 34 A4
Dean Ct. GL15 34 B1
Driffield Rd. GL15 34 C1
Fairfield Rd. GL15 34 B3
Forest Rd. GL15 34 B2
Greenways. GL15 34 A4
Grove Rd. GL15 34 A3
Hadrian Clo. GL15 34 C2
Hams Rd. GL15 34 B3
Harbour Rd. GL15 34 B6
Harrison Way. GL15 34 C4
High St. GL15 34 A4
Highfield La. GL15 34 C1
Highfield Rd. GL15 34 B3
Hill St. GL15 34 B3
Hopes Clo. GL15 34 C4

INDUSTRIAL & RETAIL:
Lydney Ind Est. GL15 34 D6
Jubilee Rd. GL15 34 C3
Julius Way. GL15 34 C2
Juno Dri. GL15 34 C3
Kimberley Clo. GL15 34 C3
Kimberley Dri. GL15 34 C2
Klondyke. GL15 34 C4
Lakeside Av. GL15 34 C4
Lakeside Dri. GL15 34 C4
Lancaster Ct. GL15 34 B1
Lancaster Dri. GL15 34 B1
Lime Way. GL15 34 B2
Livia Way. GL15 34 C3
Lych Gate Mews. GL15 34 A5
Lydfield Rd. GL15 34 B1
Lynwood Rd. GL15 34 B1
Manor Rd. GL15 34 C3
Mead La. GL15 34 A6
Meadowbank. GL15 34 C3
Minerva Walk. GL15 34 C1
Mount Pleasant. GL15 34 C4

63

Naas La. GL15 34 B3
Nero Clo. GL15 34 C2
New Rd. GL15 34 A1
Newerne St. GL15 34 B3
Nodens Way. GL15 34 C2
Oak Meadow. GL15 34 C1
Octavia Rd. GL15 34 C2
Old Furnace Clo. GL15 34 A4
Old Town Ms. GL15 34 A4
Orchard Rd. GL15 34 C4
Oxford St. GL15 34 A4
Park Ct. GL15 34 B3
Primrose Hill Rd. GL15 34 B2
Primrose Way. GL15 34 B1
Purton Pl. GL15 34 D4
Pylers Way. GL15 34 C4
Queen St. GL15 34 B2
Regent St. GL15 34 B3
Ridler Rd. GL15 34 C4
Rodley Rd. GL15 34 C3
Rodley Sq. GL15 34 C3
Rushyleaze. GL15 34 C4
Sabrina Way. GL15 34 C2
St Marys Sq. GL15 34 C3
School Cres. GL15 34 B1
Severn Rd. GL15 34 C4
Severnbank Av. GL15 34 D3
Shepherdine Clo. GL15 34 D3
South Rd. GL15 34 B2
Spring Meadow Rd.
GL15 34 B2
Springfield Rd. GL15 34 B2
Stanford Rd. GL15 34 A3
Station Rd. GL15 34 B5
Steel Av. GL15 34 C3
Steeple Vw. GL15 34 B4
Summer Leaze. GL15 34 C4
Summerleaze Rd.
GL15 34 C4
Swan Rd. GL15 34 B3
Temple Clo. GL15 34 A3
Templeway. GL15 34 A4
Templeway West.
GL15 34 A3
Tiberius Av. GL15 34 C2
The Folders. GL15 34 C3
The Orchard. GL15 34 A3
The Springs. GL15 34 B2
*The Spires,
Whitecross Rd. GL15 34 A4
Tutnalls St. GL15 34 C3
Valley Rd. GL15 34 C4
Vicarage Clo. GL15 34 B5
Victoria Rd. GL15 34 B3
Whitecross Rd. GL15 34 A4
Willow Heights. GL15 34 B1
Woodland Rise. GL15 34 B2
Wyedean Clo. GL15 34 D4
Wyntours Par. GL15 34 A4

MANGOTSFIELD

Acacia Av. BS16 35 B6
Acacia Clo. BS16 35 B6
Acacia Rd. BS16 35 B6
Albert Rd. BS16 35 C5
Alexandra Clo. BS16 35 C6
Alexandra Gdns. BS16 35 C6
Alexandra Pl. BS16 35 C6
Almond Way. BS16 35 D5
Amberley Clo. BS16 35 B2
Amberley Rd. BS16 35 B2
Avon Ring Rd. BS16 35 B1
Badminton Rd. BS16 35 C3
Baglyn Av. BS15 35 D6
Bankside. BS16 35 D5
Bath St. BS16 35 C5
Baugh Gdns. BS16 35 D1
Baugh Rd. BS16 35 D1
Beachgrove Gdns.
BS16 35 A6
Beachgrove Rd. BS16 35 A5
Beaufort Pl. BS16 35 A1
Beaufort Rd. BS16 35 C5
Beazer Clo. BS16 35 C6
Beckspool Rd. BS16 35 A1
Beechen Dri. BS16 35 A6
Beechwood Rd. BS16 35 A6
Benford Clo. BS16 35 B4
Berekley Grn. BS16 35 A1
Berekley Rd. BS16 35 C5
Bexley Rd. BS16 35 A6
Boscombe Clo. BS16 35 D2
Boscombe Cres. BS16 35 D2
Bracey Dri. BS16 35 A4

Briar Walk. BS16 35 A6
Briar Way. BS16 35 A6
Bridgeleap Rd. BS16 35 D1
Bristol Rd. BS16 35 A1
Broad St. BS16 35 C5
Broadoak Wk. BS16 35 A6
Bromley Dri. BS16 35 C1
Bromley Heath Av.
BS16 35 C2
Bromley Heath Rd.
BS16 35 B2
Brook Rd. BS16 35 A6
Bryants Clo. BS16 35 B1
Buckingham Gdns.
BS16 35 C4
Buckingham Pl. BS16 35 C4
Burley Av. BS16 35 D4
Burley Crest. BS16 35 D4
Burley Gro. BS16 35 D4
Byron Pl. BS16 35 C5
Carpenters Shop La.
BS16 35 C4
Cassell Rd. BS16 35 B5
Cave Dri. BS16 35 B3
Chapel La. BS16 35 A2
Charnell Rd. BS16 35 D5
Charnhill Cres. BS16 35 D6
Charnhill Dri. BS16 35 D6
Charnhill Vale. BS16 35 D6
Chesterfield Rd. BS16 35 D4
Chestnut Rd. BS16 35 A6
Chewton Clo. BS16 35 A6
Chine Vw. BS16 35 D2
Christchurch Av. BS16 35 C4
Christchurch La. BS16 35 C4
Church Av. BS16 35 C4
Church La. BS16 35 D1
Church Rd. BS16 35 A2
Church Vw. BS16 35 C4
Clarence Av. BS16 35 C5
Clarence Gdns. BS16 35 C5
Clarence Rd. BS16 35 C5
Cleeve Av. BS16 35 C3
Cleeve Ct. BS16 35 C3
Cleeve Hill. BS16 35 C3
Cleeve Hill Ext. BS16 35 C3
Cleeve Lawns. BS16 35 C3
Cleeve Lodge Clo. BS16 35 C3
Cleeve Lodge Rd. BS16 35 C3
Cleeve Park Rd. BS16 35 C3
Cleeve Rd,
Frenchay. BS16 35 A1
Cleeve Rd,
Mangotsfield. BS16 35 C3
Cleeve Wood Rd. BS16 35 B2
Cleve Dale. BS16 35 B2
Cleve Gdns. BS16 35 B2
Cliff Ct Dri. BS16 35 A2
Clifford Rd. BS16 35 B5
Coggan Rd. BS16 35 C6
Conifer Clo. BS16 35 B3
Coronation Rd. BS16 35 C4
Crescent Rd. BS16 35 C3
Croomes Hill. BS16 35 B4
Crossfield Rd. BS16 35 D6
Crown La. BS16 35 C6
Crownleaze. BS16 35 C6
Cunningham Gdns.
BS16 35 A4
Daubeny Clo. BS16 35 A4
Delabere Av. BS16 35 A4
Dial La. BS16 35 C4
Dodisham Wk. BS16 35 A4
Downend Pk Rd. BS16 35 C4
Downend Rd. BS16 35 A5
Downleaze. BS16 35 C2
Ducie Rd. BS16 35 C5
Eastleigh Clo. BS16 35 D6
Eastleigh Rd. BS16 35 D6
Eaton Clo. BS16 35 A5
Edgeware Rd. BS16 35 B5
Edmund Clo. BS16 35 B4
Elliott Av. BS16 35 B1
Ettrike Dri. BS16 35 A4
Fairlyn Dri. BS15 35 D6
Farm Ct. BS16 35 D3
Farm Rd. BS16 35 C3
Field Vw Dri. BS16 35 B3
Filton Rd. BS16 35 A1
Florence Rd. BS16 35 C6
Forest Way. BS16 35 A6
Four Acre Av. BS16 35 D2
Four Acre Cres. BS16 35 D1
Four Acre Rd. BS16 35 C1
Frampton Cres. BS16 35 B6
Frenchay Clo. BS16 35 A3

Frenchay
Common Rd. BS16 35 A2
Frenchay Hill. BS16 35 A2
Frenchay Rd. BS16 35 A3
Frome Side Pk. BS16 35 A3
Frome Vs. BS16 35 A2
Furze Rd. BS16 35 B6
Garnett Pl. BS16 35 D2
Gerrish Av. BS16 35 C6
Gill Av. BS16 35 A4
Glendale. BS16 35 C1
Glenside Clo. BS16 35 A3
Gloucester Rd. BS16 35 C6
Goffenton Dri. BS16 35 A6
Gorse Hill. BS16 35 A6
Grace Rd. BS16 35 B5
Graham Rd. BS16 35 D3
Grange Dri. BS16 35 B1
Grange Pk. BS16 35 B1
Grange Wood Clo.
BS16 35 B4
Greenleaze Av. BS16 35 C1
Greenleaze Clo. BS16 35 C1
Greystones. BS16 35 C1
Grove Bank. BS16 35 B1
Halbrow Cres. BS16 35 A4
Harford Dri. BS16 35 A1
Haynes La. BS16 35 B5
Hayward Rd. BS16 35 B6
Heath Ct. BS16 35 C2
Heath Gdns. BS16 35 C2
Heath Rd. BS16 35 B2
Heath Wk. BS16 35 C5
Heathcote Rd. BS16 35 C5
Heathfields. BS16 35 B2
Hermitage Rd. BS16 35 C5
High St. BS16 35 B5
Hill House Rd. BS16 35 D4
Hillfields Av. BS16 35 B6
Homestead Gdns.
BS16 35 A1
Howard Rd. BS16 35 B6
Hurstwood Rd. BS16 35 B4
Idstone Rd. BS16 35 A6
INDUSTRIAL & RETAIL:
Hayward Ind Est.
BS16 35 B6
Irving Clo. BS16 35 C6
James Clo. BS16 35 C6
James Rd. BS16 35 C6
Jubilee Rd. BS15 35 D6
Kelston Wk. BS16 35 B6
Kendall Gdns. BS16 35 B6
Kendall Rd. BS16 35 B6
Kensington Rd. BS16 35 B5
Kimberley Av. BS16 35 A5
Kimberley Clo. BS16 35 D2
Kimberley Cres. BS16 35 A5
Kimberley Rd. BS16 35 A5
Lanaway Rd. BS16 35 A4
Lawn Av. BS16 35 A5
Lawn Rd. BS16 35 A5
Leap Valley Cres. BS16 35 D2
Ledbury Rd. BS16 35 A5
Lewington Rd. BS16 35 A5
Lincombe Av. BS16 35 B4
Lincombe Rd. BS16 35 B4
Lodge Wk. BS16 35 B4
Long Clo. BS16 35 A4
Longden Rd. BS16 35 D4
Lower Station Rd.
BS16 35 B5
Lulworth Cres. BS16 35 D2
Lychet Dri. BS16 35 D2
Lydney Rd. BS16 35 C5
Malmains Dri. BS16 35 A1
Mangotsfield Rd. BS16 35 D5
Manor Pl. BS16 35 A1
Marlborough Dri. BS16 35 A1
Marshfield Park. BS16 35 B2
Marshfield Rd. BS16 35 A6
Maywood Av. BS16 35 A5
Maywood Cres. BS16 35 A5
Maywood Rd. BS16 35 A5
Meadow Clo. BS16 35 D2
Middle Rd. BS15 35 D6
Midland Rd. BS16 35 B5
Millward Gro. BS16 35 A5
Morley Clo. BS16 35 C6
Morley Rd. BS16 35 C6
Narrow La. BS16 35 C6
Nelson Rd. BS16 35 B5
North St. BS16 35 C5
North Vw, Upper
Soundwell. BS16 35 B6
North Vw,
Staple Hill. BS16 35 D5

Northcote Rd. BS16 35 D4
Oakdale Av. BS16 35 C2
Oakdale Clo. BS16 35 C2
Oakdale Ct. BS16 35 C2
Oakdale Rd. BS16 35 C2
Overndale Rd. BS16 35 B4
Overnhill Ct. BS16 35 B5
Overnhill Rd. BS16 35 B4
Overnhurst Ct. BS16 35 B4
Page Clo. BS16 35 D5
Page Rd. BS16 35 B5
Park Cres. BS16 35 B1
Park Rd. BS16 35 C4
Parkhurst Av. BS16 35 A6
Peach Rd. BS16 35 D4
Pemberton Ct. BS16 35 B5
Pendennis Av. BS16 35 B5
Pendennis Rd. BS16 35 B5
Pendock Rd. BS16 35 A3
Penn Dri. BS16 35 B1
Pilgrims Wy. BS16 35 C2
Pleasant Rd. BS16 35 B5
Portland Pl. BS16 35 B6
Portland St. BS16 35 B6
Prattens La. BS16 35 B5
Quakers Clo. BS16 35 C1
Quakers Rd. BS16 35 C1
Quarry Rd. BS16 35 A2
Queensholme Av.
BS16 35 C1
Queensholme Clo.
BS16 35 C1
Queensholme Cres.
BS16 35 C1
Queensholme Rd. BS16 35 C1
Radley Rd. BS16 35 A5
Railway Ter. BS16 35 B6
Riverside Dri. BS16 35 A3
Riverwood Rd. BS16 35 B1
Riviera Cres. BS16 35 C6
Rockland Rd. BS16 35 B3
Rockside Av. BS16 35 D1
Rodway Vw. BS15 35 D6
Ronayne Wk. BS16 35 A4
Rose Wk. BS16 35 B6
Rosedale Rd. BS16 35 A6
Salisbury Gdns. BS16 35 C4
Salisbury Rd. BS16 35 C4
Sandholme Clo. BS16 35 A4
Sandringham Av. BS16 35 C1
Sandringham Pk. BS16 35 C2
Saunders Rd. BS16 35 C5
Selbrooke Cres. BS16 35 A3
Seymour Rd. BS16 35 C5
Shepherds Clo. BS16 35 C5
Sheppard Rd. BS16 35 A4
Shimsey Clo. BS16 35 B4
Shrubbery Rd. BS16 35 B4
Sidelands Rd. BS16 35 B3
Signal Rd. BS16 35 D6
Soundwell Rd. BS16 35 D5
South Vw. BS16 35 D5
Southernhay. BS16 35 B6
Stanbridge Clo. BS16 35 D4
Stanbridge Rd. BS16 35 D3
Stanbury Av. BS16 35 A5
Stanley Pk Rd. BS16 35 C6
Staplehill Rd. BS16 35 A5
Station Rd. BS15 35 D6
Summerleaze. BS16 35 B6
Sunridge. BS16 35 B4
Sutherland Av. BS16 35 D2
Symington Rd. BS16 35 A5
Teewell Av. BS16 35 C6
Teewell Clo. BS16 35 D5
Teewell Hill. BS16 35 D5
Tern Rd. BS16 35 C5
The Common. BS16 35 A2
The Crescent. BS16 35 B6
The Croft. BS16 35 D4
The Gardens. BS16 35 C6
The Park. BS16 35 A1
The Rosery. BS16 35 A6
Thicket Av. BS16 35 A6
Thicket Rd. BS16 35 B5
Tuckett La. BS16 35 A2
Tylers La. BS16 35 B6
Uplands Rd. BS16 35 B6
Upper Station Rd.
BS16 35 B5
Urfords Dri. BS16 35 B3
Valley Gdns. BS16 35 D2
Victoria St. BS16 35 C5
Wadham Dri. BS16 35 A1
Wedgewood Rd. BS16 35 C1

Wellington Pk. BS16 35 A1
Wenmore Clo. BS16 35 C1
West Park Rd. BS16 35 C5
Westbourne Rd. BS16 35 D2
Westerleigh Rd. BS16 35 D3
White Lodge Rd. BS16 35 D6
Whittington Rd. BS16 35 A3
Windsor Ct. BS16 35 C3
Woodhall Clo. BS16 35 D3
Woodlands Rise. BS16 35 B3
Woodside Rd. BS16 35 B2
Wrenbert Rd. BS16 35 B5
York Rd. BS16 35 C5

MICKLETON

Alveston Grange. GL55 36 A4
Arbour Clo. GL55 36 A2
Back La. GL55 36 A2
Bakers Hill. GL55 36 A3
Ballards Clo. GL55 36 A2
Bearcroft Gdns. GL55 36 A1
Broad Marston Rd.
GL55 36 A1
Broadway Rd. GL55 36 A3
Campden Rd. GL55 36 A3
Cedar Rd. GL55 36 B1
Chapel La. GL55 36 A2
Cotswold Edge. GL55 36 A2
Garden Clo. GL55 36 A2
Gloucester La. GL55 36 A2
Granbrook La. GL55 36 B1
Greyrick Ct. GL55 36 A2
High St. GL55 36 A2
Inverlea Ct. GL55 36 A1
Meon Rd. GL55 36 B1
Mill La. GL55 36 B1
Norton View. GL55 36 A2
Nursery Clo. GL55 36 A2
Old Manor Gdns. GL55 36 B2
Orchard Clo. GL55 36 B1
Pound La. GL55 36 A2
Stratford Rd. GL55 36 B1
Wheatfield Ct. GL55 36 A1

MITCHELDEAN

Abenhall Rd. GL17 36 B6
Ash Gro. GL17 36 B4
Barton Hill. GL17 36 D5
Baynham Rd. GL17 36 B5
Bradley Ct Rd. GL17 36 C4
Brook St. GL17 36 C5
Carisbrook Rd. GL17 36 D4
Churchill Way. GL17 36 B5
Colchester Clo. GL17 36 B6
Court Farm La. GL17 36 C5
Dean Meadows. GL17 36 C5
Deansway Rd. GL17 36 D4
Eastern Av. GL17 36 C5
Glebe Clo. GL17 36 B4
Gloucester Rd. GL17 36 C6
Hawker Hill. GL17 36 C5
High St. GL17 36 C5
Hill View Clo. GL17 36 C1
Holywell Rd. GL17 36 B4
INDUSTRIAL & RETAIL:
Ladygrove
Business Pk. GL17 36 D6
Rank Xerox
Business Pk. GL17 36 C4
May Meadow La. GL17 36 B5
New Rd. GL17 36 B6
New St. GL17 36 B5
Nourse Pl. GL17 36 B6
Oakhill Rd. GL17 36 C4
Old Dean Rd. GL17 36 B4
Orchard Clo. GL17 36 B5
Parks Rd. GL17 36 C5
Platts Row. GL17 36 B4
Ross Rd. GL17 36 B4
St Michaels Clo. GL17 36 B5
Silver St. GL17 36 B6
Stars Pitch. GL17 36 C5
Stenders Rd. GL17 36 B5
Talbot Pl. GL17 36 B5
The Bullring. GL17 36 B5
The Crescent. GL17 36 B4
The Stenders. GL17 36 C5
Townsend. GL17 36 B6
Tusculum Way. GL17 36 B5
Walwyn Clo. GL17 36 B6
Wintles Clo. GL17 36 B6

64

MORETON-IN-MARSH

Bourton Rd. GL56 37 A2
Bowes Lyon Clo. GL56 37 A3
Bowling Green. GL56 37 A1
Corders La. GL56 37 C2
Cotsmore Clo. GL56 37 C2
Croft Holm. GL56 37 C2
Davies Rd. GL56 37 C2
Dulverton Pl. GL56 37 B2
East St. GL56 37 A2
Errington. GL56 37 C2
Evenlode Gdns. GL56 37 C3
Evenlode Rd. GL56 37 C2
Fosseway Av. GL56 37 A3
Fosseway Clo. GL56 37 B3
Fosseway Dri. GL56 37 A3
Grays La. GL56 37 B2
Harvard Clo. GL56 37 C2
High St. GL56 37 A2
Hospital Rd. GL56 37 A2
Jamieson Ct. GL56 37 A3
Keble Rd. GL56 37 B3
London Rd. GL56 37 B2
*Mead Clo, St Georges
    Clo. GL56 37 B2
Mosedale. GL56 37 C1
New Rd. GL56 37 B2
Nursery Clo. GL56 37 B1
Oriel Gro. GL56 37 B3
Oxford St. GL56 37 A2
Parkers La. GL56 37 A2
Primrose Ct. GL56 37 B2
Ralph Ct. GL56 37 B3
Redesdale Pl. GL56 37 A3
St Davids Ct. GL56 37 B2
St Davids Walk. GL56 37 B2
St Edwards Ct. GL56 37 A3
St Georges Clo. GL56 37 B2
St James Ct. GL56 37 A3
St Pauls Ct. GL56 37 A3
St Peters Ct. GL56 37 A3
Sawkey Gro. GL56 37 B3
Station Rd. GL56 37 B2
Stockwells. GL56 37 B2
Stow Rd. GL56 37 A3
Swan Clo. GL56 37 A2
Tinkers Clo. GL56 37 B3
The Green. GL56 37 B2
Warneford Pl. GL56 37 B2
Wellington Rd. GL56 37 C2

NAILSWORTH/ MINCHINHAMPTON

Avening Rd. GL6 38 C5
Badgers Way. GL6 38 A4
Barn Clo. GL6 38 B5
Barnfield Av. GL6 38 A4
Barnfield Rd. GL6 38 A4
Bath Rd,
    Nailsworth. GL6 38 B6
Bath Rd,
    Woodchester. GL5 38 A1
Bell La. GL6 39 G2
Besbury La. GL6 39 F1
Besbury Park. GL6 39 H2
Blue Boys Park. GL6 39 G2
Box Cres. GL6 39 F3
Box La. GL6 38 D3
Brewery La. GL6 38 C5
Bridge St. GL6 38 C4
Brimscombe Hill. GL5 39 E1
Bunting Hill. GL6 38 A5
Bunting Way. GL6 38 A4
Burfords Grnd. GL6 38 A5
Burleigh La. GL5 39 E1
Burleigh Vw. GL5 39 F1
Burma Rd. GL6 38 A4
Butcher Mills La,
    Market St. GL6 38 C5
Butt St. GL6 38 C5
Cambridge Way. GL6 39 F2
Carters Way. GL6 38 A4
Cecil Ct. GL6 39 G2
Chapel Hill. GL5 38 C1
Chapel La. GL6 39 G3
Cherrytree Clo. GL6 38 A4
Chestnut Clo. GL6 38 B5
Chestnut Hill. GL6 38 B5
Church La. GL5 38 C2

Church Rd. GL5 38 A3
Church St. GL5 38 C5
Churchill Clo. GL6 38 B5
Churchill Rd. GL6 38 B4
Cirencester Rd. GL6 39 E2
Colliers Wood. GL6 38 A4
Convent La. GL5 38 A1
Cow La. GL5 38 A2
Cuckoo Row. GL6 39 F3
Culver Hill. GL5 38 B1
Dark La. GL6 38 B5
Deans Quarry. GL5 39 F1
Dr Browns Clo. GL6 39 F2
Dr Browns Rd. GL6 39 F2
Dr Crawfords Clo. GL6 39 F3
Dunkirk Pitch. GL5 38 B3
Eastfield Rd. GL6 39 H1
Everest Clo. GL6 39 E2
Fairview Clo. GL6 38 C4
Fewster Rd. GL6 38 B5
Fewster Sq. GL6 38 B5
Fieldways. GL6 38 A4
Firs Rd. GL6 38 C4
Fountain St. GL6 38 C5
Foxes Dell. GL6 38 A4
Friday St. GL6 39 G3
Frogmarsh La. GL5 38 A1
*Frying Pan Alley,
    Fewster Rd. GL6 38 B5
George St. GL6 38 C5
Glebe Rd. GL6 39 H2
Grange Clo. GL6 39 F2
Gunbarrel Alley. GL6 38 C5
Gydynap La. GL5 38 B2
Hanover Gdns. GL6 38 C5
Hawthorn Ridge. GL6 38 A3
Hayes Rd. GL6 38 B4
Hiatt Rd. GL6 39 F2
High St. GL6 39 G3
Higher Newmarket Rd.
    GL6 38 A5
Highcroft. GL6 38 A5
Homefield. GL6 38 A5
Horsley Rd. GL6 38 B6
Inchbrook Rd. GL6 38 A3
INDUSTRIAL & RETAIL:
Inchbrook
    Trading Est. GL5 38 B2
Merretts Mill
    Ind Centre. GL5 38 B1
Nailsworth
    Trading Est. GL6 38 D5
Springmill Ind Est.
    GL6 39 E5
Jubilee Rd. GL6 38 B4
Kings St. GL6 39 G3
Lawnside. GL6 38 A4
Love La. GL6 39 F1
Lower Newmarket Rd.
    GL6 38 A5
Manor Clo. GL6 39 F2
Market Sq. GL6 39 G3
Market St. GL6 38 C5
Marling Clo. GL5 38 C1
Middle Tynings. GL6 38 B4
Moffat Rd. GL6 38 B4
New Rd. GL6 39 F3
Newmarket Rd. GL6 38 A5
Northfields Rd. GL6 38 B4
Norton Ridge. GL6 38 A3
Nortonwood. GL6 38 A4
Nympsfield Rd. GL6 38 A4
Old Bristol Rd. GL6 38 B6
Old Common. GL6 39 H2
Old Market. GL6 38 C5
Old School Clo. GL6 38 B4
Ollney Rd. GL6 39 F2
Orchard Mead. GL6 38 A2
Park La. GL5 38 A2
Park Rd. GL6 38 C5
Park Rd Cres. GL6 38 C5
Park Ter. GL6 39 F3
Parsons Ct. GL6 39 G3
Pensile Rd. GL6 38 B5
Pike La. GL6 38 B5
Plumbers La. GL6 38 A6
Ragnal La. GL6 38 A6
Ricardo Rd. GL6 39 F2
Ringfield Clo. GL6 38 C5
Rowan Way. GL6 38 A3
St Chloe La. GL6 38 B1
St Chloe Mead. GL5 38 B1
St Chloes Grn. GL5 38 B1
St Marys Hill. GL5 38 A2
Scar Hill. GL6 39 G2
School Rd. GL6 39 G2
Sevenacres Rd. GL6 38 A5

Shears Pitch. GL6 38 C4
Sheppard Way. GL6 39 F2
Shortwood Rd. GL6 38 A5
Simmonds Ct. GL6 39 G3
Snakes La. GL6 38 B3
Southfield. GL6 39 F3
Spring Hill. GL6 38 B5
Springhill Clo. GL6 38 C5
Springhill Cres. GL6 38 C5
Star Hill. GL6 38 A4
Station Rd. GL6 38 C4
Stroud Rd. GL6 38 B3
Summersfield Clo. GL6 39 H2
Summersfield Rd. GL6 39 H2
Syon Rd. GL6 39 H2
Tabrams Pitch. GL6 38 C5
Tetbury La. GL6 38 C6
Tetbury St. GL6 39 G3
The Bulwarks. GL6 39 H2
The Glebe. GL6 39 G2
The Knapp. GL6 39 G2
The Ladder. GL6 38 C4
The Pen. GL6 39 E4
The Ridings. GL6 38 C6
The Rollers. GL6 38 B5
The Roundabouts. GL6 39 F1
The Tynings. GL6 39 H2
Theescombe Hill. GL5 38 B2
Theescombe La. GL6 38 B1
Tobacconist Rd. GL6 39 G3
Tooke Rd. GL6 39 E2
Trinity Dri. GL6 39 H2
Tynings Rd. GL6 38 B4
Upper Hayes Rd. GL6 38 B4
Upper Park Rd. GL6 38 C5
Upper Tynings. GL6 38 B4
Watledge Bank. GL6 38 C4
Watledge Rd. GL6 38 B2
Well Hill. GL6 39 F3
West End. GL6 39 F3
West Tynings. GL6 38 B5
Wheelwrights Cnr. GL6 38 B3
Whips La. GL6 38 B3
Whitecroft. GL6 38 B4
Windmill Rd. GL6 39 E2
Windsoredge La. GL6 38 A3
Woefuldane Bottom.
    GL6 39 H3
Wood La. GL6 38 C5
Woodpecker Walk.
    GL6 38 A4
Worley Ridge. GL6 38 B5

NEWENT

Akermans Orchard.
    GL18 37 B6
Ash Tree Clo. GL18 37 C6
Ayland Clo. GL18 37 D5
Blenheim Dri. GL18 37 D6
Bradfords Clo. GL18 37 A6
Bradfords La. GL18 37 A6
Bridge St. GL18 37 B4
Broad St. GL18 37 B5
Brookside. GL18 37 B6
Bury Bar La. GL18 37 C5
Chedworth. GL18 37 C5
Church St. GL18 37 C5
Church Way. GL18 37 C5
Cleeve Rise. GL18 37 D6
Coopers Way. GL18 37 D6
Court La. GL18 37 C5
Court Rd. GL18 37 C5
Craddock Rd. GL18 37 B6
Croft Clo. GL18 37 D5
Croft Rd. GL18 37 D5
Culver St. GL18 37 B6
Foley Rd. GL18 37 C6
Friars Walk. GL18 37 B5
Furnace La. GL18 37 B4
Gardeners Way. GL18 37 B5
Glebe Clo. GL18 37 B5
Glebe Ct. GL18 37 B5
Glebe Rd. GL18 37 A5
Glebe Way. GL18 37 B5
Gloucester St. GL18 37 C5
Graces Pitch. GL18 37 C5
Greenways. GL18 37 B5
Hartland. GL18 37 D5
High St. GL18 37 B5
Hills View. GL18 37 B5
Holts Rd. GL18 37 B5
Horsefair La. GL18 37 A4

INDUSTRIAL & RETAIL:
Town Farm Ind Est.
    GL18 37 D5
Johnstone Rd. GL18 37 B6
Knights Cres. GL18 37 A6
Knights Way. GL18 37 B5
Lakeside. GL18 37 B5
Market Sq. GL18 37 C5
Newlands Ct. GL18 37 D5
Old Maids Walk. GL18 37 B5
Old Station Rd. GL18 37 B4
Onslow Rd. GL18 37 A6
Peacock Gdns. GL18 37 B6
Perry Clo. GL18 37 C5
Pippin Clo. GL18 37 C6
Redmarley La. GL18 37 C4
Reevers Rd. GL18 37 B5
Robinson Clo. GL18 37 B5
Ross Rd. GL18 37 A5
Rosset Way. GL18 37 C6
St Bartholomews.
    GL18 37 C5
Sheppard Way. GL18 37 D5
Tewkesbury Rd. GL18 37 B4
The Butts. GL18 37 C5
The Crease. GL18 37 C5
The Crofts. GL18 37 C5
The Tythings. GL18 37 A6
Tythings Mews. GL18 37 B6
Vauxhall. GL18 37 A5
Watery La. GL18 37 A6
West View. GL18 37 B5
Whittington Wk. GL18 37 C5
Winfield. GL18 37 B6

PAINSWICK

Ashwell. GL6 40 C2
Berry Clo. GL6 40 C2
Bisley St. GL6 40 D2
Blakewell Mead. GL6 40 C1
Butt Green. GL6 40 C1
Canton Acre. GL6 40 D1
Castle Clo. GL6 40 C3
Cheltenham Rd. GL6 40 D2
Churchill Way. GL6 40 C2
Cotswold Mead. GL6 40 C3
Court Orchard. GL6 40 C3
Edge La. GL6 40 A2
Edge Rd. GL6 40 B2
Friday St. GL6 40 D2
Gloucester Rd. GL6 40 D1
Golf Course Rd. GL6 40 D1
Greenhouse La. GL6 40 D3
Gyde Rd. GL6 40 D3
Hale La. GL6 40 D3
Hambutts Dri. GL6 40 C2
Hambutts Mead. GL6 40 D2
Hollyhock La. GL6 40 D2
Hyett Clo. GL6 40 C2
Hyett Orchard. GL6 40 D2
Kemps La. GL6 40 D3
Kingsmead. GL6 40 C2
Kingsmill La. GL6 40 C3
Knap La. GL6 40 D3
Lower Washwell La.
    GL6 40 D2
New St. GL6 40 C2
Orchard Mead. GL6 40 D3
Pullens Rd. GL6 40 D1
Queens Mead. GL6 40 C3
Randalls Field. GL6 40 D1
St Marys St. GL6 40 D2
Stamages La. GL6 40 C3
Stroud Rd. GL6 40 B3
*The Churns,
    Hale La. GL6 40 D3
The Croft. GL6 40 C2
The Highlands. GL6 40 D1
Tibbiwell. GL6 40 D2
Tibbiwell La. GL6 40 D2
Upper Washwell. GL6 40 D1
Vicarage St. GL6 40 D2
Victoria St. GL6 40 D2
Whitehorse La. GL6 40 D2
Woodborough Clo.
    GL6 40 D3

ST. BRIAVELS

Barrowell La. GL15 41 C2
Bream Rd. GL15 41 D2
Castle Cres. GL15 41 C2

Cinder Hill. GL15 41 B2
Cross Keys. GL15 41 D2
Crown La. GL15 41 C2
East St. GL15 41 C1
Hewelsfield La. GL15 41 C2
High St. GL15 41 C2
Lower Rd. GL15 41 B3
Mork Rd. GL15 41 C1
Park Clo. GL15 41 C2
Pystol La. GL15 41 C2
St Annes Way. GL15 41 C2
St Bruels Clo. GL15 41 C2
Sandy La. GL15 41 B3
Smithville Clo. GL15 41 D2
Smithville Pl. GL15 41 D1
The Square. GL15 41 C1
Townsend Clo. GL15 41 D2

SEDBURY

*Albion Sq,
    Thomas St. NP16 42 C3
Arlington Ct. NP16 42 E3
Bank St. NP16 42 C3
Beachley Rd. NP16 42 D1
*Beauford Sq,
    High St. NP16 42 C3
Beech Gro. NP16 42 B4
Bigstone Clo. NP16 42 D1
Bigstone Gro. NP16 42 D1
Bridge St. NP16 42 C2
Bridget Dri. NP16 42 E4
Bulwark Rd. NP16 42 B3
Buttington Rd. NP16 42 E3
Buttington Ter. NP16 42 F4
Caird St. NP16 42 C3
Castle Gdns. NP16 42 B2
Castle View. NP16 42 D2
Castleford Gdns. NP16 42 C1
Castleford Hill. NP16 42 C1
Church Rd. NP16 42 C2
Church Row. NP16 42 C2
Cliff View. NP16 42 E4
Coleford Rd. NP16 42 D1
Danes Clo. NP16 42 B3
*Davis Ct,
    Bridge St. NP16 42 C2
Deans Gdns. NP16 42 A2
Deans Hill. NP16 42 B3
Dell View. NP16 42 C3
Denmark Dri. NP16 42 E4
Edmond Rd. NP16 42 E2
Elm Clo. NP16 42 E1
Elm Rd. NP16 42 D1
Elmdale. NP16 42 C2
Exmouth Pl. NP16 42 C3
Fair View. NP16 42 B4
Fairfield Rd. NP16 42 C4
Fitzosborne Clo. NP16 42 B3
Garden City Way.
    NP16 42 C3
Gloucester Rd. NP16 42 D1
Grahamstown Gro.
    NP16 42 E2
Grahamstown Rd.
    NP16 42 E3
Green St. NP16 42 C3
Gwentlands Clo. NP16 42 B4
Gwy Ct. NP16 42 C2
Hanover Clo. NP16 42 A2
Hanover Ct. NP16 42 B4
Hardwick Av. NP16 42 C3
Hardwick Hill. NP16 42 C3
Hardwick Hill La. NP16 42 B3
Hardwick Ter. NP16 42 B3
Hendrick Dri. NP16 42 C4
High Beech La. NP16 42 A4
High St. NP16 42 B3
High View. NP16 42 B3
Hilltop. NP16 42 B4
Hocker Hill St. NP16 42 C2
Hollins Clo. NP16 42 C2
Howells Row. NP16 42 D2
Hughes Cres. NP16 42 C4
Huntfield Rd. NP16 42 A2
Kendall Sq. NP16 42 C2
King Alfreds Rd. NP16 42 E4
Kingsmark La. NP16 42 A2
Lancaster Way. NP16 42 B2
Larkfield Av. NP16 42 B4
Larkfield Pk. NP16 42 B4
Larkhill Clo. NP16 42 B4
*Library Pl,
    Bank St. NP16 42 C3
Lower Church St. NP16 42 C2

Madocke Rd. NP16 42 E3
*Manor Way,
Bank St. NP16 42 C3
Marten Rd. NP16 42 C4
Mathern Rd. NP16 42 B4
Meadow Wk. NP16 42 B3
Mercian Way. NP16 42 E4
Middle St. NP16 42 C2
Mill La. NP16 42 C3
*Montague Almshouse,
Upr Church St.
NP16 42 C2
Moor St. NP16 42 C3
Mopla Rd. NP16 42 C1
Mount Pleasant. NP16 42 B3
Mount Way. NP16 42 B2
Mounton Clo. NP16 42 B3
Mounton Dri. NP16 42 B3
Mounton Rd. NP16 42 A3
Myrtle Pl. NP16 42 D2
Nelson St. NP16 42 C3
Newport Rd. NP16 42 B4
Normandy Way. NP16 42 A2
Norse Way. NP16 42 E3
Oakfield Av. NP16 42 A2
Offas Clo. NP16 42 E3
Old Bulwark Rd. NP16 42 B4
Orchard Clo. NP16 42 C2
Orchard Farm Clo.
NP16 42 E4
Ormerod Rd. NP16 42 E3
Park View,
Chepstow. NP16 42 A2
Park View,
Sedbury. NP16 42 F3
Penda Pl. NP16 42 E3
Penterry Park. NP16 42 A3
Piercefield Av. NP16 42 A2
Port Wall. NP16 42 C3
Portwall Rd. NP16 42 C3
Priory Clo. NP16 42 B2
Regent Way. NP16 42 B3
Restway Wall. NP16 42 C3
*Riflemans Way,
Bank St. NP16 42 C3
River Vw. NP16 42 C3
Rockwood Clo. NP16 42 B2
Ruffetts Clo. NP16 42 B3
St Andrews Av. NP16 42 C4
St Anns St. NP16 42 C2
St Davids Clo. NP16 42 C4
St Georges Rd. NP16 42 C4
St Johns Gdns. NP16 42 A2
St Kingsmark Av. NP16 42 B2
St Lawrence La. NP16 42 A4
St Lawrence Pk. NP16 42 A3
St Lawrence Rd. NP16 42 A2
St Marys St. NP16 42 C2
St Maur Gdns. NP16 42 B2
St Tecla Rd. NP16 42 C4
St Tewdric Rd. NP16 42 B4
Saxon Pl. NP16 42 E3
School La. NP16 42 C3
Sedbury La. NP16 42 E2
Severn Av. NP16 42 D2
Severn Cres. NP16 42 C3
Silleys Clo. NP16 42 D1
Station Rd. NP16 42 C3
Steep St. NP16 42 B3
Strongbow Rd. NP16 42 C4
Stuart Clo. NP16 42 B2
Tallards Pl. NP16 42 E3
Tempest Way. NP16 42 A3
The Back. NP16 42 D2
The Martins. NP16 42 E2
The Myrtles. NP16 42 C1
The Old Hill. NP16 42 C2
The Paddock. NP16 42 B4
The Priory. NP16 42 C2
The Yetts. NP16 42 B3
*Thomas Powis Almshouses,
Bridge St. NP16 42 C2
Thomas St. NP16 42 C3
Tudor Dri. NP16 42 A2
Turnike Clo. NP16 42 A2
Tuts Hill Gdns. NP16 42 D2
Tylers Way. NP16 42 E3
Upper Church St. NP16 42 C2
Upper Nelson St. NP16 42 C3
Vauxhall La. NP16 42 B3
Vauxhall Rd. NP16 42 B3
Warwick Clo. NP16 42 B4
Waters Rd. NP16 42 C3
Welsh St. NP16 42 A1
Wintour Clo. NP16 42 A2
Wirewood Clo. NP16 42 D1
Wirewood Cres. NP16 42 D1

Wye Cres. NP16 42 C4
Wye Valley
Link Rd. NP16 42 B4
Wyebank Av. NP16 42 D2
Wyebank Clo. NP16 42 D3
Wyebank Cres. NP16 42 D3
Wyebank Pl. NP16 42 D3
Wyebank Rise. NP16 42 E3
Wyebank Rd. NP16 42 D3
Wyebank View. NP16 42 E3
Wyebank Way. NP16 42 D3

SHURDINGTON

Atherton Clo. GL51 43 B2
Badgeworth La. GL51 43 A2
Bishop Rd. GL51 43 B2
Blenheim Orchard.
GL51 43 C1
Church La. GL51 43 B2
Cowls Mead. GL51 43 B2
Farm La. GL51 43 B3
Greenway Clo. GL51 43 B3
Greenway La. GL51 43 B3
Gwinnett Ct. GL51 43 C2
Harrison Rd. GL51 43 B3
Lambert Av. GL51 43 A3
Lambert Clo. GL51 43 B2
Lambert Dri. GL51 43 B2
Lambert Gdns. GL51 43 B3
Lambert Ter. GL51 43 B2
Laurence Clo. GL51 43 B2
Lawn Cres. GL51 43 C2
Leckhampton La. GL51 43 C2
Marsh Ter. GL51 43 B2
Robertson Rd. GL51 43 B2
School La. GL51 43 B3
Shurdington Rd. GL51 43 B3
Sinclair Rd. GL51 43 B2
The Orchard Gro. GL51 43 B3
Vicarage Clo. GL51 43 C2
Whitelands La. GL51 43 B3
Wilson Rd. GL51 43 B2
Yarnolds. GL51 43 B2

SOUTH CERNEY

Beaverstone Clo. GL7 41 B6
Beaverstone Rd. GL7 41 B6
Berkeley Clo. GL7 41 C5
Bow Wow. GL7 41 C5
Boxbush Clo. GL7 41 C5
Boxbush Rd. GL7 41 C5
Broadway La. GL7 41 C5
Church La. GL7 41 B5
Churn Clo. GL7 41 B5
Clarks Way. GL7 41 B5
Edwards College. GL7 41 B4
Field Clo. GL7 41 C5
Ham La. GL7 41 C6
High St. GL7 41 B6
Huxley Ct. GL7 41 C5
Jubilee Gdns. GL7 41 B5
Kingfisher Pl. GL7 41 C5
Lakeside. GL7 41 D5
Langet. GL7 41 B5
Meadow Way. GL7 41 C5
Mill Clo. GL7 41 C5
Oak Way. GL7 41 C6
Paymans Ter. GL7 41 B5
River Way. GL7 41 B5
Robert Franklin Way.
GL7 41 D5
School La. GL7 41 B5
Silver St. GL7 41 B4
Station Rd. GL7 41 C5
Sudeley Dri. GL7 41 B6
The Close. GL7 41 C5
The Leaze. GL7 41 B6
The Lennards. GL7 41 C5
The Limes. GL7 41 C5
The Paddock. GL7 41 B5
Timbrells Clo. GL7 41 B5
Wildmoorway La. GL7 41 D5
Willow Gro. GL7 41 C5

STONEHOUSE

Abbots Way. GL10 46 C6
Adelaide Gdns. GL10 46 C3
Albany. GL10 46 C3

Aldergate St. GL10 46 D5
Anderson Dri. GL10 46 D5
Arrowsmith Dri. GL10 46 C3
Avenue Ter. GL10 46 B5
Barlow Clo. GL10 46 B5
Bath Rd. GL10 46 C5
Blackbird Ct. GL10 46 D4
Boakes Dri. GL10 46 B5
Bramble La. GL10 46 D4
Bridgend Ct. GL10 46 D4
Brisbane . GL10 46 C3
Bristol Rd. GL10 46 A4
Browns La. GL10 46 D6
Brunel Way. GL10 46 A4
Burdett. GL10 46 B5
Burdett Clo. GL10 46 D5
Canberra. GL10 46 C3
Cedar Gdns. GL10 46 D4
Chaffinch Clo. GL10 46 D4
Chapel Row. GL10 46 C5
Chestnut Av. GL10 46 C4
Church La. GL10 46 B5
Coates Gdns. GL10 46 D4
College View. GL10 46 D5
Cotswold Grn. GL10 46 D4
Crescent Clo. GL10 46 C6
Crescent Rd. GL10 46 C6
Crest Ct. GL10 46 D4
Downton Rd. GL10 46 C6
Ebley By-Pass. GL10 46 D6
Ebley Rd. GL10 46 D6
Elms Rd. GL10 46 C4
Festival Rd. GL10 46 B5
Glen Ct. GL10 46 D4
Glenthorne Clo. GL10 46 D3
Gloucester Rd. GL10 46 C4
Green St. GL10 46 C4
Grosvenor Rd. GL10 46 C3
Haven Av. GL10 46 D4
High St. GL10 46 C4
Juniper Way. GL10 46 D4
Kestrel Clo. GL10 46 D4
Kimmins Rd. GL10 46 D4
Kings Rd. GL10 46 C3
Laburnum Mews. GL10 46 C5
Laburnum Rd. GL10 46 C5
Laburnum Walk. GL10 46 C5
Magpie Ct. GL10 46 D4
Meadow Rd. GL10 46 C4
Meadway Rd. GL10 46 C6
Melbourne Clo. GL10 46 C3
Melbourne Dri. GL10 46 C3
Midland Rd. GL10 46 B4
Nasted La. GL10 46 A3
Nursery Ter. GL10 46 C6
Oak Way. GL10 46 D5
Oldends La. GL10 46 A5
Orchard Ct. GL10 46 C5
Orchard Pl. GL10 46 C5
Osprey Dri. GL10 46 D4
Paddock Rise. GL10 46 D4
Park Par. GL10 46 C4
Park Rd. GL10 46 B5
Partridge Clo. GL10 46 D4
Pearcroft Rd. GL10 46 D6
Perth. GL10 46 C3
Pheasant Mead. GL10 46 D4
Queens Rd. GL10 46 C5
Quietways. GL10 46 C5
Regent St. GL10 46 C5
Robin Ct. GL10 46 D4
Rosedale Av. GL10 46 D5
Ryelands Clo. GL10 46 C4
Ryelands Rd. GL10 46 C4
St Cyrils Rd. GL10 46 D5
Severn Rd. GL10 46 B4
Sherborne Ct. GL10 46 D4
Starling Ct. GL10 46 D4
Stonedale Rd. GL10 46 B4
Storrington Pl. GL10 46 D5
Storrington Rd. GL10 46 D5
Sydney. GL10 46 C3
The Lawns. GL10 46 C4
The Square. GL10 46 C4

Upper Queens Rd.
GL10 46 D5
Verney Rd. GL10 46 D5
Wharfedale Way. GL10 46 C6
Whitefield Clo. GL10 46 C6
Willow Rd. GL10 46 D5
Woodcock Clo. GL10 46 B5
Woodcock La. GL10 46 C4

STOW-ON-THE-WOLD

Back Walls. GL54 43 B5
Bailey Clo. GL54 43 C5
Bartletts Park. GL54 43 B6
Camp Gdns. GL54 43 B5
Chamberlayne Clo.
GL54 43 B6
Chapel St. GL54 43 B5
Church St. GL54 43 B5
Clifton Clo. GL54 43 B5
Digbeth St. GL54 43 B5
Evesham Rd. GL54 43 A4
Fisher Clo. GL54 43 B6
Fosse Folly. GL54 43 B4
Fosse La. GL54 43 B4
Fosseway. GL54 43 B5
Glebe Clo. GL54 43 B5
Griffin Clo. GL54 43 D5
High St. GL54 43 B5
Jubilee Clo. GL54 43 B5
King Georges Field.
GL53 43 C5
Lower Park St. GL54 43 B5
Markét Sq. GL54 43 B5
Maugersbury Pk. GL54 43 B6
Mount Pleasant Clo.
GL53 43 C5
Oakleys Clo. GL54 43 C5
Oddington Rd. GL54 43 C5
Park St. GL54 43 B5
St Edwards Dri. GL54 43 B5
St Edwards Rd. GL54 43 B5
Sheep St. GL54 43 B6
Shepherds Row. GL54 43 B5
Shepherds Way. GL54 43 B5
Station Rd. GL54 43 B6
Sterling Clo. GL54 43 C5
Talbot Cotts. GL54 43 B5
Talbot Ct. GL54 43 B5
Talbot Sq. GL54 43 B5
The Courtyard. GL54 43 B4
The Park. GL54 43 B4
The Stables. GL54 43 B4
Union St. GL54 43 B5
Well La. GL54 43 B4

STROUD

Acre St. GL5 45 E5
All Saints Rd. GL5 45 E4
Allen Dri. GL5 44 B4
Archway Gdns. GL5 44 B4
Arundel Dri. GL5 44 B6
Arundel Mill La. GL5 45 E6
Barrowfield Rd. GL5 44 B3
Bath Rd. GL5 44 B6
Bath St. GL5 44 D5
Beards La. GL5 44 B5
Bedford St. GL5 44 D5
Beeches Grn. GL5 44 D4
Belle Vue Clo. GL5 44 B5
Belle Vue Rd. GL5 45 E5
Belmont Rd. GL5 45 F6
Birches Clo. GL5 45 E4
Birches Dri. GL5 44 D4
Bisley Old Rd. GL5 45 E5
Bisley Rd. GL5 45 E5
Bowbridge La. GL5 45 E6
Brewery Yd. GL5 44 A5
Briar Clo. GL5 45 E3
Brick Row. GL5 45 E5
Bridge Side. GL5 44 A6
Bridge St. GL5 44 C6
Burford Dri. GL5 44 B4
Byron Rd. GL5 44 B4
Cainscross Rd. GL5 44 A5
Capel Ct. GL5 45 E4
Captain Barton Clo.
GL5 45 F4
Cashes Green Rd. GL5 44 A5
Castle Pitch. GL5 45 E6
Castle Rise. GL5 45 E6

Castle St. GL5 45 E5
Castlemead Rd. GL5 44 C6
Catherines St. GL5 45 F5
Catswood Ct. GL5 45 F3
Central Rd. GL5 44 B5
Chapel St. GL5 45 E5
Cheapside. GL5 44 D5
Chestnut La. GL5 44 B5
Church St. GL5 44 D5
Churchfield Rd. GL5 45 F6
Clare Ct. GL5 45 F5
College Rd. GL5 44 B4
Cornhill. GL5 44 D5
Coronation St. GL5 44 C6
Cotswold Rd. GL5 44 A4
Cotteswold Rise. GL5 45 E5
Cowle Rd. GL5 45 E6
Cutler Rd. GL5 45 E4
Daisy Bank. GL5 45 F6
Daniels Rd. GL5 45 G5
Delmont Gro. GL5 44 D4
Dr Newtons Way. GL5 44 D5
Downfield. GL5 44 B4
Downfield Rd. GL5 44 B5
Dudbridge Hill. GL5 44 B6
Dudbridge Rd. GL5 44 A6
Duderstadt St. GL5 44 B4
Elm Rd. GL5 44 A4
Far Leazes. GL5 45 E5
Farmhill Cres. GL5 44 B3
Farmhill La. GL5 44 B4
Farrs La. GL5 44 D5
*Fawkes Pl,
Bedford St. GL5 44 D5
Ferndale Rd. GL6 44 B1
Field Rd,
Rodborough. GL5 44 C6
Field Rd, Stroud. GL5 45 E6
Field Rd,
Whiteshill. GL6 44 B2
Folly La. GL5 44 D4
Folly Rise. GL5 45 E3
Fort View Ter. GL5 44 A6
Frome Av. GL5 44 C6
Frome Gdns. GL5 44 A6
Frome Hall La. GL5 44 C6
Frome Park Rd. GL5 44 B6
Fromeside. GL5 44 D6
Gannicox Rd. GL5 44 D5
George St. GL5 44 D5
Gibson Clo. GL5 45 G5
Gloucester St. GL5 44 D5
Grange View. GL5 45 E4
Grove Park Rd. GL5 45 E4
Heathfield Rd. GL5 44 B3
Heazle Pl. GL5 44 D4
High St. GL5 44 D5
Highfield Rd,
Stroud. GL5 45 F6
Highfield Rd,
Whiteshill. GL6 44 B1
Hill Top Clo. GL5 45 G5
Hillfield. GL5 44 B5
Hillier Clo. GL5 45 F3
Hollow La. GL5 45 E5
Horns Rd. GL5 45 E6
Humphreys Clo. GL5 44 A4
Hyett Rd. GL5 44 A5
INDUSTRIAL ESTATES:
Lightpill Trading Est.
GL5 44 C6
Salmon Springs
Depot. GL6 45 E4
John Bevan Clo. GL5 45 E4
John St. GL5 44 B3
Keats Gdns. GL5 44 B3
Kendrick St. GL5 44 D5
Kilminster Rd. GL5 45 G5
King St. GL5 44 D5
Kingley Rd. GL5 44 A5
Kings Rd. GL5 44 C6
Knapp La. GL5 45 H2
Langtoft . GL5 45 F5
Lansdown. GL5 44 D5
Leazes Pitch. GL5 45 E5
Libbys Dri. GL5 45 E4
Lightwood La. GL5 44 A1
Locking Hill. GL5 44 C5
Lodgemore Clo. GL5 44 C5
Lodgemore La. GL5 44 B5
Lovedays Mead. GL5 44 D4
Lower Churchfield Rd.
GL5 45 F6
Lower Kitesnest La.
GL6 44 B1
Lower Leazes. GL5 45 E5

Lower Spillmans. GL5 44 C6
Lower St, Stroud. GL5 45 E6
Lower St,
Whiteshill. GL6 44 B1
Main Rd. GL6 44 B1
Maldon Ter. GL5 44 D5
Maple Dri. GL5 44 B3
Marling Cres. GL5 44 A4
Mason Rd. GL5 45 G5
Mathews Way. GL5 44 B4
Meadow La West. GL5 44 A6
Meadow Way. GL5 44 A6
Merrywalks. GL5 44 D5
Middle Hill. GL5 45 F5
Middle Leazes. GL5 45 E5
Middle Spillmans. GL5 44 C6
Middle St,
Stroud Hill. GL5 45 E5
Middle St,
Uplands. GL5 45 E4
Mill Farm Dri. GL5 44 A4
Milton Gro. GL5 45 F5
Moor Hall Pl. GL5 44 A4
Mosley Cres. GL5 44 A5
Mosley Rd. GL5 44 A4
Nelson St. GL5 45 E5
Northfield Mews. GL5 45 E4
Nouncells Cross. GL5 45 F5
Nursery Clo. GL5 45 E6
Oak Dri. GL5 44 A4
Paganhill Est. GL5 44 A4
Paganhill La. GL5 44 A5
Painswick Old Rd. GL5 44 D4
Painswick Rd. GL5 44 C3
Park End Rd. GL5 44 A3
Park Rd. GL5 45 E6
Park View Dri. GL5 44 A4
Parliament Ct. GL5 45 E5
Parliament St. GL5 45 E5
Paynes Pl. GL5 44 B6
Peghouse Clo. GL5 45 F3
Peghouse Rise. GL5 45 E3
Queens Dri. GL5 44 A4
Queens Rd. GL5 44 C6
Reservoir Clo. GL5 45 G5
Reservoir Rd. GL5 45 F5
Ridgemont Rd. GL5 45 F6
Rodborough Av. GL5 44 C6
Rodborough Hill. GL5 44 C6
Row Croft. GL5 44 D5
Rowcroft Retreat. GL5 44 D5
Russell St. GL5 44 D5
Rye Lease Clo,
Rye Lease Rd. GL5 45 E5
Rye Lease Rd. GL5 45 E5
St Brendans Rd. GL5 45 E5
Selsley Hill. GL5 44 A6
Shepherds Clo. GL5 45 E4
Shepherds Croft. GL5 45 E4
Shooters End. GL5 44 D4
Slad La. GL5 45 G4
Slad Rd. GL5 44 D5
Slade Brook. GL5 45 F4
Spider La. GL5 45 F6
Spillmans Rd. GL5 44 C6
Spring La. GL5 45 E6
Springfield Rd. GL5 45 E5
Stanton Rd. GL5 44 A4
Station Rd. GL5 44 D5
Strachans Clo. GL5 44 B5
Stratford Rd. GL5 44 B4
Streamside. GL5 45 E5
Summer Clo. GL5 45 F5
Summer Cres. GL5 45 E5
Summer St. GL5 45 E5
Sutton Pl Gdns. GL5 45 E5
Swifts Hill View. GL5 45 F3
Sycamore Clo. GL5 45 E4
Target Clo. GL5 45 G5
The Budding. GL5 45 F3
The Circle. GL5 45 E4
The Hill. GL5 44 C5
The Plain. GL6 44 B2
The Shambles. GL5 44 D5
The Square. GL5 45 E4
The Woodlands. GL5 45 E4
Thompson Rd. GL5 45 E4
Threadneedle St. GL5 44 D5
Trinity Rd. GL5 45 E6
Union St. GL5 44 D5
Uplands Rd. GL5 45 E4
Upper Kitesnest La.
GL6 44 B1
Upper Leazes. GL5 45 E5
Upper Springfield Rd.
GL5 45 E4
Valley View Rd. GL5 45 G6

Victory Rd. GL6 44 B1
Wades La. GL6 44 D1
Wall Bridge. GL5 44 D5
Well End. GL5 45 F4
Wesley Ct. GL5 45 E5
West Ct Grange. GL5 44 D4
Westward Rd. GL5 44 A6
Wheelers Walk. GL5 44 B4
White Hall. GL5 45 E5
Whitehouse Park. GL5 44 A5
Wickridge Clo. GL5 45 E4
Woodhouse Dri. GL5 44 D6
Woodlands Dri. GL5 45 F4

TETBURY

Alexander Gdns. GL8 47 D2
Bartley Croft. GL8 47 D2
Bath Rd. GL8 47 C4
Beech Tree Gdns. GL8 47 D2
Berkeley Way. GL8 47 D1
Berrells Rd. GL8 47 C4
Black Horse Hill. GL8 47 C3
Blind La. GL8 47 D1
Braybrooke Clo. GL8 47 E2
Chantry Ct. GL8 47 D3
Charlton Rd. GL8 47 B3
Chavenage La. GL8 47 B1
Cherry Orchard Rd.
GL8 47 D2
Chestnut Clo. GL8 47 C2
Cheviot Clo. GL8 47 D1
Chipping Steps. GL8 47 D3
Chipping St. GL8 47 D3
Church St. GL8 47 D3
Cirencester Rd. GL8 47 D3
Clarrie Rd. GL8 47 D1
Close Gdns. GL8 47 C3
Combers End. GL8 47 D2
Conygar Rd. GL8 47 D1
Cook Spool. GL8 47 D2
Coronation Rd. GL8 47 C1
Cotswold Clo. GL8 47 D1
Cottons La. GL8 47 C2
Court Field. GL8 47 C2
Cutwell. GL8 47 C3
Eccles Ct. GL8 47 D3
Elizabeth Gdns. GL8 47 C2
Five Trees Ct. GL8 47 C2
Fox Hill. GL8 47 C3
Gastrall Ct. GL8 47 D2
Grange La. GL8 47 C4
Grove Gdns. GL8 47 C1
Gumstool Hill. GL8 47 D3
Hampton St. GL8 47 C1
Herd La. GL8 47 E3
Highfield Rd. GL8 47 C1
Hodges Clo. GL8 47 D2
Holder Clo. GL8 47 D2
Hookhouse La. GL8 47 A4
INDUSTRIAL & RETAIL:
Hampton St Ind Est.
GL8 47 B1
Priory Ind Est. GL8 47 D2
Tetbury Ind Est. GL8 47 E2
The Old Quarry
Ind Units. GL8 47 D1
Jacobs Clo. GL8 47 D1
Linfoot Rd. GL8 47 C3
London Rd. GL8 47 D2
Long St. GL8 47 C3
Longfurlong La. GL8 47 B4
Longtree Clo. GL8 47 C1
Love La. GL8 47 D3
Lowfield Rd. GL8 47 C1
Magdalen Rd. GL8 47 C2
Malthouse Walk. GL8 47 D2
Market Pl. GL8 47 D3
New Church St. GL8 47 D3
New Leaze Gdns. GL8 47 D3
Newnton Rd. GL8 47 D3
Northfield Clo. GL8 47 E2
Northfield Rd. GL8 47 D2
Northleaze. GL8 47 E2
Northlands Way. GL8 47 D1
Old Brewery La. GL8 47 D3
Oxleaze Clo. GL8 47 C2
Oxleaze Rd. GL8 47 C2
Park Vw. GL8 47 D2
Priory Way. GL8 47 D2
Quail Meadows. GL8 47 C2
Romney Rd. GL8 47 C1
Ryland Clo. GL8 47 D2
St Marys Rd. GL8 47 C2
Shepherds Mead. GL8 47 D1

Sherwood Rd. GL8 47 C3
Silver St. GL8 47 D3
Southfield. GL8 47 C4
Springfields. GL8 47 E2
Starveal La. GL8 47 C4
Suffolk Clo. GL8 47 D1
Talboys Walk. GL8 47 D1
The Berrells. GL8 47 C4
The Chipping. GL8 47 D3
The Damsels. GL8 47 D2
The Ferns. GL8 47 D3
The Green. GL8 47 D3
Upton Gdns. GL8 47 C1
Wains Ct. GL8 47 D3
Webb Rd. GL8 47 C3
West St. GL8 47 C3
Wheat Hill. GL8 47 C2
Windsor Rd. GL8 47 C2
Wistaria Rd. GL8 47 C2
Woodward Clo. GL8 47 C1

TEWKESBURY

Abbots Rd. GL20 48 B6
Abbots Walk. GL20 48 A5
Alexandra Way. GL20 49 G3
Alpha Clo. GL20 49 E3
Arundel Rd. GL20 48 C2
Ash Rd. GL20 49 G2
Ashchurch Rd. GL20 48 C4
Avon View. GL20 48 D2
Back of Avon. GL20 48 B4
Barton Ct. GL20 48 C4
Barton Mews. GL20 48 B4
Barton Rd. GL20 48 B4
Barton St. GL20 48 B4
Battle Rd. GL20 48 A6
Beaufort Pl. GL20 48 B6
Bellflower Rd. GL20 48 D6
Beta Clo. GL20 49 F2
Bevan Gdns. GL20 49 H1
Bishops Walk. GL20 48 B3
Bowler Rd. GL20 49 H1
Bramley Rd. GL20 48 C3
Bredon Rd. GL20 48 B3
Brensham Rd. GL20 49 E3
Brookside. GL20 48 D2
Cambrian Rd. GL20 48 C5
Canterbury Leys. GL20 48 D3
Carrant Rd. GL20 48 C3
Cedar Rd. GL20 49 G2
Chance St. GL20 48 B4
Cherry Orchard. GL20 49 H2
Church St. GL20 48 A4
Churchill Gro. GL20 48 D4
Clarence Rd. GL20 48 B6
Clifford Av. GL20 48 C6
*Collins Ct,
Back of Avon. GL20 48 B4
*Comptons Alley,
Barton St. GL20 48 B4
Cormorant Av. GL20 48 C5
Conigree La. GL20 48 B6
Cotswold Gdns. GL20 48 C3
Cotteswold Rd. GL20 48 B3
Coventry Clo. GL20 48 B6
Cromers Clo. GL20 49 G1
Curlew Clo. GL20 49 G1
Cypress Rd. GL20 48 C6
Delta Dri. GL20 49 E3
Derwent Dri. GL20 48 D2
Despenser Rd. GL20 48 B5
Devonshire Pl. GL20 48 B6
Digby Rd. GL20 48 C2
East St. GL20 48 B4
Elm Rd. GL20 49 H2
Elmbury Dri. GL20 48 C3
Elmvil Rd. GL20 48 B3
Fairway. GL20 49 G2
Farm Clo. GL20 49 G2
*Fletchers Alley,
Barton St. GL20 48 B4
Folly Gdns. GL20 48 B4
Foresters Pl. GL20 48 B5
Gadwell Rd. GL20 48 C5
Gander La. GL20 48 A4
Gannaway La. GL20 48 A4
George Dowty Dri.
GL20 49 G1
Gloucester Rd. GL20 48 A5
Gould Dri. GL20 49 G2
Grange Ct. GL20 49 H2
Grange Rd. GL20 49 H1
Gravel Walk. GL20 48 B3
Green La. GL20 49 E3

Greylag Cres. GL20 48 C5
Greystone Clo. GL20 48 D2
Gupshill Clo. GL20 48 B6
*Hanover Ct,
Back of Avon. GL20 48 B4
Harbour View. GL20 48 B2
Harbourside. GL20 48 B2
Hardwick Bank Rd.
GL20 49 G1
Harrier Clo. GL20 48 D5
Hastings Pl. GL20 48 B6
Hawthorn Way. GL20 49 H1
Heaver Clo. GL20 48 C5
High St. GL20 48 B4
Hollams Rd. GL20 48 B3
Holm Oak Clo. GL20 48 C6
Hone Ct. GL20 48 B4
Howard Clo. GL20 49 G2
Howard Rd. GL20 49 G2
Howells Rd. GL20 49 H1
*Hughes Alley,
Barton St. GL20 48 B4
Hughes Clo. GL20 49 H1
INDUSTRIAL & RETAIL:
Ashchurch Ind Est.
GL20 49 F3
Northway Trading Est.
GL20 49 H3
Tewkesbury Business
Centre. GL20 49 F3
Tewkesbury
Ind Est. GL20 49 E3
Jeynes Row. GL20 48 B3
Kestrel Way. GL20 49 G1
King Johns Ct. GL20 48 B3
Kings Gate. GL20 49 E3
Kingston Rd. GL20 49 G2
Knights Way. GL20 48 D4
Lancaster Rd. GL20 48 B6
Lanes Ct. GL20 48 B4
Lapwing Clo. GL20 49 G1
Laurel Av. GL20 48 C6
Lee Rd. GL20 49 H2
*Lilleys Alley,
Barton St. GL20 48 B4
Lime Rd. GL20 48 C6
Lincoln Clo. GL20 48 A6
Lincoln Green La. GL20 48 A6
Link Rd. GL20 48 D2
Long Eights. GL20 49 G2
Longtown Rd. GL20 48 A6
Lower Lode La. GL20 48 A5
Manor Park. GL20 48 D2
Manor Pl. GL20 48 B6
Margaret Rd. GL20 48 B5
Maxstoke Clo. GL20 48 C6
Meadow Clo. GL20 48 D4
Mill St. GL20 48 A4
Milne Pastures. GL20 49 E3
Mitton Way. GL20 48 C2
Monkey Meadow.
GL20 49 G1
Monterey Clo. GL20 48 C6
Moulder Rd. GL20 48 D4
*Mount Pleasant Rd,
Barton St. GL20 48 B4
Mythe Rd. GL20 48 A2
*Naylor Ct,
Back of Avon. GL20 48 B4
Nelson St. GL20 48 B4
Neville Rd. GL20 48 B5
Newtown La. GL20 48 D3
Northway La. GL20 48 D3
Oak Dri. GL20 49 G2
Old Manor La. GL20 48 D2
*Old Post Office La,
Oldbury. GL20 48 B4
Oldbury Rd. GL20 48 B4
Oldfield. GL20 48 B4
Orchard Ct. GL20 48 B4
Palm Rd. GL20 48 C6
Park Clo. GL20 49 G1
Peach Clo. GL20 48 C6
Priors Alley. GL20 48 A4
*Priors Ct,
Back of Avon. GL20 48 B4
Pyke Rd. GL20 48 D4
Quay St. GL20 48 B3
Queens Rd. GL20 48 B3
Red La. GL20 48 B3
Redwood Clo. GL20 49 H2
Richard Pl. GL20 48 B4
Richmond Rd. GL20 48 C6
Robin Clo. GL20 49 G1
Ropewalk. GL20 48 B3
Rosefield Cres. GL20 48 D4
Saffron Rd. GL20 48 B4

*St Andrews Clo,
St Davids Rd. GL20 49 H3
St Davids Rd. GL20 49 H3
*St Georges Rd,
St Davids Rd. GL20 49 H3
St Marys La. GL20 48 A4
St Marys Rd. GL20 48 A4
*St Patricks Rd,
St Davids Rd. GL20 49 H3
Sallis Clo. GL20 49 G1
Seymour Pl. GL20 48 B5
*Shakespeare Ct,
Back of Avon. GL20 48 B4
Shannon Way. GL20 49 E3
Shephard Mead. GL20 48 A5
Sinderberry Dri. GL20 49 H1
Smiths La. GL20 48 B3
Snowdonia Rd. GL20 48 C5
Somerset Clo. GL20 48 B6
Spa Gdns. GL20 48 D4
Springfield. GL20 48 D3
Stanford Rd. GL20 49 G2
Stanton Rd. GL20 48 C2
Station La. GL20 48 C3
Station Rd. GL20 48 B3
Station St. GL20 48 B3
Steward Rd. GL20 49 G2
Stokes Ct. GL20 48 B4
Sun St. GL20 48 B4
Swilgate Rd. GL20 48 B4
Sycamore Rd. GL20 49 G2
Tawny Clo. GL20 49 F1
Tewkesbury Rd. GL20 48 D1
Thatcham Rd. GL20 48 C6
The Apple Orchard.
GL20 49 G1
The Hopyard. GL20 49 G1
The Park. GL20 49 G1
The Pear Orchard.
GL20 49 G1
The Sandfield. GL20 49 G2
Theocs Clo. GL20 48 A6
Thistle Downs. GL20 49 G1
Tirle Bank Way. GL20 48 D4
Tolsey La. GL20 48 B4
Tretawn Gdns. GL20 48 D4
Trinity St. GL20 48 B4
Troughton Pl. GL20 48 D4
Tudor Pl. GL20 48 B6
Tug Wilson Clo. GL20 49 G1
Twixtbears. GL20 48 B3
Virginia Clo. GL20 49 H2
Virginia Rd. GL20 49 H2
Wagtail Dri. GL20 49 G1
Wakeman Clo. GL20 48 C6
Walkley Rd. GL20 48 C6
Walls Ct. GL20 48 B4
Walton Gdns. GL20 49 E4
Warren Rd. GL20 49 G2
Warwick Pl. GL20 48 B5
Watledge Clo. GL20 48 B4
Well Clo. GL20 49 G2
Wellfield. GL20 49 E3
Wenlock Rd. GL20 48 B5
Westfield Av. GL20 49 G2
Wheatstone Clo. GL20 49 G1
Willis Walk. GL20 49 G1
Wynyards Clo. GL20 48 C4
*Yarnells Alley,
Barton St. GL20 48 B4
York Rd. GL20 48 B6

THORNBURY

Alexandra Way. BS35 50 B3
Armstrong Clo. BS35 50 C5
Ashgrove. BS35 50 C5
Avon Way. BS35 50 C6
Bath Rd. BS35 50 B5
Blakes Rd. BS35 50 D6
Bockenem. BS35 50 D6
Brookmead. BS35 50 C6
Brunel Way. BS35 50 B6
Buckingham Par. BS35 50 B4
Butts La. BS35 50 B2
Castle Coombe. BS35 50 B4
Castle Ct. BS35 50 B5
Castle St. BS35 50 A4
Catsbrain La. BS35 50 D1
Celandine Clo. BS35 50 D3
Chantry Rd. BS35 50 B4
Chapel St. BS35 50 C2
Charles Clo. BS35 50 C2
Chatsworth Pk. BS35 50 C6
Cherwell Clo. BS35 50 C6

Chestnut Dri. BS35 50 C4
Cheviot Dri. BS35 50 D5
Chiltern Vw. BS35 50 D6
Church Rd. BS35 50 A4
Clare Walk. BS35 50 B4
Cleveland Dri. BS35 50 D5
Colin Clo. BS35 50 B5
Colne Sq. BS35 50 C6
Combermere. BS35 50 C5
Coombe Av. BS35 50 B4
Cooper Rd. BS35 50 B4
Cossham Clo. BS35 50 C3
Crispin La. BS35 50 B5
Crossways Rd. BS35 50 D4
Cumbria Clo. BS35 50 C4
Dean Av. BS35 50 D6
Derwent Ct. BS35 50 D6
Dovedale. BS35 50 D6
Dyrham Clo. BS35 50 C2
Eastbury Clo. BS35 50 C4
Eastbury Rd. BS35 50 C4
Eastland Av. BS35 50 B4
Eastland An. BS35 50 B4
Eastland Rd. BS35 50 B4
Easton Hill Rd. BS35 50 C4
Elizabeth Clo. BS35 50 D5
Ellesmere. BS35 50 C5
Elmdale Cres. BS35 50 C5
Eskdale. BS35 50 C6
Falcon Way. BS35 50 C5
Finch Clo. BS35 50 C3
Foxglove Clo. BS35 50 D4
Frome Ct. BS35 50 B5
Fulmar Clo. BS35 50 C3
Gillingstool. BS35 50 B5
Gloucester Rd. BS35 50 B4
Grovesend Rd. BS35 50 C5
Hacket La. BS35 50 D4
Hamble Clo. BS35 50 C5
Hatchmere. BS35 50 C5
Hawthorne Cres. BS35 50 C4
Hazel Cres. BS35 50 C4
High St. BS35 50 A6
Hillbrook Rd. BS35 50 D5
Hillcrest. BS35 50 B5
Homefield. BS35 50 C5
Hopkin Clo. BS35 50 B5
Horse La. BS35 50 D1
Howard Rd. BS35 50 B3
Hyde Av. BS35 50 B3
Jubilee Dri. BS35 50 D5
Kempton Clo. BS35 50 B2
Kennet Way. BS35 50 D5
Kensington Clo. BS35 50 B3
Kestrel Clo. BS35 50 C4
Kingfisher Clo. BS35 50 D3
Kington Clo. BS35 50 A5
Knapp Rd. BS35 50 C5
Ladden Ct. BS35 50 C6
Larkspur Clo. BS35 50 D4
Lavender Clo. BS35 50 D3
Mallow Clo. BS35 50 D3
Malvern Dri. BS35 50 D6
Manor Walk. BS35 50 B2
Maple Av. BS35 50 C4
Meadowside. BS35 50 C5
Medina Ct. BS35 50 C6
Medway Ct. BS35 50 D6
Midland Rd. BS35 50 B5
Midland Way. BS35 50 D6
Millfields. BS35 50 B3
Millfields Clo. BS35 50 B3
Morton St. BS35 50 C1
Morton Way. BS35 50 C2
Nightingale Clo. BS35 50 D3
North East Rd. BS35 50 C3
North Rd. BS35 50 C4
Oakleaze Rd. BS35 50 A1
Oldbury La. BS35 50 A1
Orchard Av. BS35 50 C5
Orchard Grange. BS35 50 A4
Osprey Pk. BS35 50 D3
Park Rd. BS35 50 B3
Park View Rd. BS35 50 C4
Parkland Way. BS35 50 B2
Pentland Dri. BS35 50 D5
Pine Clo. BS35 50 B5
Pittville Clo. BS35 50 C2
Primrose Clo. BS35 50 D3
Prowse Clo. BS35 50 B4
Pulling Grn. BS35 50 B5
Quaker La. BS35 50 B5
Queens Walk. BS35 50 B2
Rabley Rd. BS35 50 B4
Raglan Pl. BS35 50 B5
Regent Clo. BS35 50 B3
Ribblesdale. BS35 50 C6

Rock St. BS35 50 B5
Rosslyn Way. BS35 50 B2
St Davids Rd. BS35 50 B5
St John St. BS35 50 B5
St Marys Rd. BS35 50 B5
St Marys Way. BS35 50 B5
Sawmill La. BS35 50 B5
Severn Dri. BS35 50 B4
Severn View Rd. BS35 50 C3
Shannon Ct. BS35 50 D6
Short Way. BS35 50 B6
Sibland. BS35 50 D5
Sibland Clo. BS35 50 D5
Sibland Rd. BS35 50 D5
Sibland Way. BS35 50 C5
Solent Way. BS35 50 D6
Sorrel Clo. BS35 50 D4
Speedwell Clo. BS35 50 D3
Spey Clo. BS35 50 C5
Springfield. BS35 50 C5
Squires Leaze. BS35 50 C3
Stafford Cres. BS35 50 B4
Stokefield Clo. BS35 50 A4
Streamleaze. BS35 50 B5
Streamside Walk. BS35 50 B5
Swallow Pk. BS35 50 C2
Sycamore Dri. BS35 50 C4
Tamar Clo. BS35 50 D6
The Paddocks. BS35 50 C5
The Plain. BS35 50 C4
Thicket Walk. BS35 50 C4
Tiling Rd. BS35 50 B4
Trent Dri. BS35 50 D6
Tyndale View. BS35 50 B5
Upper Bath Rd. BS35 50 B5
Victoria Clo. BS35 50 B3
Vilner La. BS35 50 B6
Walker Way. BS35 50 B6
Walnut Clo. BS35 50 C4
Warwick Pl. BS35 50 A4
Waterford Clo. BS35 50 D6
Wharfedale. BS35 50 C6
Whitfield Rd. BS35 50 C3
Windrush Ct. BS35 50 C6
Woodleigh. BS35 50 C4
Wye Ct. BS35 50 C6

UPPER LYDBROOK

Camomile Grn. GL17 51 B5
Church Hill. GL17 51 B3
Church Rd. GL17 51 B3
Church View. GL17 51 B3
Coppice Rd. GL17 51 A2
Eddys La. GL17 51 D1
Edwards Clo. GL17 51 B2
Forest Rd. GL17 51 B4
Forge Hill. GL17 51 A1
Greenfield Clo. GL17 51 B2
Greenfield Rd. GL17 51 B2
Hatton Clo. GL17 51 B5
High Row. GL17 51 A2
High St. GL17 51 D2
Highbeech Rd. GL17 51 D2
Hillside Ter. GL17 51 B2
Horselea. GL17 51 B2
Joys Green Rd. GL17 51 B2
Mill Row. GL17 51 A1
New Rd. GL17 51 A6
Orchard Rd. GL17 51 B2
Probertsbarn La. GL17 51 A2
Ridge Pl. GL17 51 B6
Rocks Rd. GL17 51 A2
School Cres. GL17 51 B2
School Rd,
  Joys Green. GL17 51 B2
School Rd, Upper
  Lydbrook. GL17 51 B4
Squires Rd. GL17 51 A4
The Bourts. GL17 51 B5
Uphill Rd. GL17 51 B4
Valley Rd. GL17 51 B6
Vention La. GL17 51 B6
Woodland View. GL17 51 B3
Worral Hill. GL17 51 B6
Wye View Rd. GL17 51 B2

WINCHCOMBE

Abbey Ter. GL54 52 B3
Abbots Leys Rd. GL54 52 A3

Back La. GL54 52 B3
Barksdale. GL54 52 A3
Barnmeadow Rd. GL54 52 A2
Bassett Clo. GL54 52 B1
Bicks La. GL54 52 C2
Binyon Rd. GL54 52 A3
Blenheim Ct. GL54 52 B2
Broadway Rd. GL54 52 C2
Brook Clo. GL54 52 A3
Bull La. GL54 52 C2
Castle St. GL54 52 C3
Cedar Gro. GL54 52 B1
Chandos St. GL54 52 C2
Cheltenham Rd. GL54 52 A3
Clarendon Rd. GL54 52 B1
Cow La. GL54 52 B2
Crispin Clo. GL54 52 B1
Crispin Rd. GL54 52 B1
Delavale Rd. GL54 52 B1
Dents Ter. GL54 52 B3
Eldersfield Clo. GL54 52 B1
Farmcote Gdns. GL54 52 A2
Gervase Rd. GL54 52 B1
Gillette Clo. GL54 52 B3
Gloucester St. GL54 52 B3
Godwin Rd. GL54 52 B1
Greenways. GL54 52 C1
Greet Rd. GL54 52 B1
Gretton Rd. GL54 52 B1
Hailes St. GL54 52 C2
Harveys La. GL54 52 A3
High St. GL54 52 C3
Huddlestone Rd. GL54 52 B1
Kenelm Rise. GL54 52 B1
Kenulf Rd. GL54 52 C2
Kyderminster Clo.
  GL54 52 B1
Langley Clo. GL54 52 B3
Langley Rd. GL54 52 A3
Malthouse La. GL54 52 B3
Mercia Rd. GL54 52 B2
Mill La. GL54 52 A3
North St. GL54 52 C2
Norton Clo. GL54 52 B1
Orchard Rd. GL54 52 B2
Puck Pit La. GL54 52 D1
Rathmore Clo. GL54 52 C1
Riverside. GL54 52 C1
Rushley La. GL54 52 B2
St Peters Way. GL54 52 B2
Seymour Pl. GL54 52 B2
Silk Mill La. GL54 52 C3
Spittle Leys. GL54 52 B2
Stancombe. GL54 52 C2
Stancombe La. GL54 52 D2
Stancombe View. GL54 52 C2
Summers Rd. GL54 52 B2
The Hyde. GL54 52 A3
Tobacco Clo. GL54 52 A3
Vineyard St. GL54 52 B3
Whitmore Rd. GL54 52 B1
Wincel Rd. GL54 52 C1

WINTERBOURNE/ FRAMPTON COTTERELL

Abbeydale. BS36 53 B3
Adams Land. BS36 53 F2
Alexandra Rd. BS36 53 F2
Badminton Rd. BS36 53 E4
Barley Clo. BS36 53 E1
Barton Clo. BS36 53 A4
Beaufort Rd. BS36 53 D1
Beaver Clo. BS36 53 C2
Beesmoor Rd. BS36 53 E2
Bell Rd. BS36 53 E3
Blackberry Dri. BS36 53 E3
Boundary Rd. BS36 53 F2
Bourne Clo. BS36 53 B2
Bradley Av. BS36 53 A4
Bradstone Rd. BS36 53 A4
Branksome Dri. BS36 53 A3
Bridge Way. BS36 53 E1
Bristol Rd. BS36 53 A2
Brockridge La. BS36 53 D1
Brookside Dri. BS36 53 D1
Burghley Clo. BS36 53 B4
Burrough Way. BS36 53 A4
Butterfield Clo. BS36 53 B1
Camberley Dri. BS36 53 B1
Cannons. BS36 53 C2
Cedars Way. BS36 53 A4
Church Clo. BS36 53 E1

Church La, Frampton
  Cotterell. BS36 53 F3
Church La,
  Winterbourne. BS36 53 A3
Church Rd. BS36 53 C1
Cloisters Rd. BS36 53 B3
Clyde Rd. BS36 53 E1
Common Rd. BS36 53 B2
Court Rd. BS36 53 B1
Crossley Clo. BS36 53 B2
Crossman Av. BS36 53 A4
Dawley Clo. BS36 53 B2
Deacon Clo. BS36 53 A4
Dormer Clo. BS36 53 F3
Downfield Dri. BS36 53 A4
Dragon Rd. BS36 53 A4
Englands Cres. BS36 53 B2
Factory Rd. BS36 53 C2
Fernleaze. BS36 53 F3
Fire Engine La. BS36 53 F2
Flaxpits La. BS36 53 A3
Footes La. BS36 53 E2
Fox Rd. BS36 53 D1
Frampton End Rd.
  BS36 53 F1
Friary Grange Park.
  BS36 53 A3
Frome View. BS36 53 D2
Frome Way. BS36 53 B4
Gazzard Clo. BS36 53 A2
Gazzard Rd. BS36 53 B2
Gladstone La. BS36 53 E2
Gledemoor Dri. BS36 53 F2
Goose Grn. BS36 53 E1
Green Dragon Rd.
  BS36 53 A4
Green La. BS36 53 A2
Harcombe Rd. BS36 53 A4
Harris Barton. BS36 53 D2
Hazel Gro. BS36 53 A4
Heath Clo. BS36 53 F4
Heath Gdns. BS36 53 F4
Heathcote Dri. BS36 53 F2
Heather Av. BS36 53 D3
Henfield Rd. BS36 53 F4
Hicks Common Rd.
  BS36 53 A4
High St. BS36 53 A3
Hillside Clo. BS36 53 F2
Hillside La. BS36 53 E2
Hither Mead. BS36 53 E2
Holmwood Clo. BS36 53 A3
Huckford Rd. BS36 53 A4
Kelbra Rise. BS36 53 D3
Langthorn Clo. BS36 53 F2
Larkfield. BS36 53 F2
Lewton La. BS36 53 B2
Linden Clo. BS36 53 A3
Lower Chapel La. BS36 53 A4
Lower Stone Clo. BS36 53 F1
Ludwell Clo. BS36 53 A4
Main View. BS36 53 F2
Manor Clo. BS36 53 E3
Manor La. BS36 53 C2
Marsh Clo. BS36 53 A4
Masons View. BS36 53 B3
Matford Clo. BS36 53 B4
Meadow Mead. BS36 53 D1
Meadow View. BS36 53 F2
Medway Dri. BS36 53 D3
Mill Clo. BS36 53 E3
Mill La, Frampton
  Cotterell. BS36 53 E2
Mill La,
  Frampton End. BS36 53 D1
*Millennium Clo,
  Alexandra Rd. BS36 53 F2
Mount Clo. BS36 53 C1
Mount Cres. BS36 53 A4
Newlands Av. BS36 53 F3
Nicholls La. BS36 53 A4
Nightingale Clo. BS36 53 D3
North Rd. BS36 53 F3
Oakleaze. BS36 53 F3
Oldlands Av. BS36 53 F3
Orchard Clo. BS36 53 B3
Orchard Rd. BS36 53 F2
Park Av, Frampton
  Cotterell. BS36 53 D3
Park Av,
  Winterbourne. BS36 53 B3
Park La. BS36 53 D3
Park Row. BS36 53 D1
Parkside Av. BS36 53 A3
Pendock Rd. BS36 53 B4
Prospect Clo. BS36 53 C1

Prospect La. BS36 53 C1
Ram Hill. BS36 53 F4
Rathbone Clo. BS36 53 E4
Rectory Rd. BS36 53 A3
Ridgeway. BS36 53 F2
Ridings Rd. BS36 53 E3
Robel Av. BS36 53 E3
Rockside Gdns. BS36 53 E1
Rose La. BS36 53 F3
Roundways. BS36 53 F3
Rushton Dri. BS36 53 F2
Ryecroft Rd. BS36 53 E1
Rylestone Clo. BS36 53 C1
St Annes Dri. BS36 53 F4
St Francis Rd. BS36 53 B3
St Michaels Clo. BS36 53 B3
St Peters Cres. BS36 53 E2
St Saviours Rise. BS36 53 D3
Salem Rd. BS36 53 E3
Sallys Way. BS36 53 B2
School Rd. BS36 53 B1
South View. BS36 53 B3
South View Cres. BS36 53 F3
South View Rise. BS36 53 F3
Stanford Clo. BS36 53 B1
Star Barn Rd. BS36 53 E2
Station Rd. BS36 53 E4
Sunnyside. BS36 53 E2
Swan La. BS36 53 A2
The Brake. BS36 53 E4
The Causeway. BS36 53 F2
The Close. BS36 53 E3
The Gully. BS36 53 C2
The Land. BS36 53 F2
The Orchard. BS36 53 F2
The Ridge. BS36 53 F2
The Ridings. BS36 53 E3
The Spinney. BS36 53 D2
Thornhayes Clo. BS36 53 C1
Upper Chapel La. BS36 53 E2
Upper Stone Clo. BS36 53 F2
Vicarage Rd. BS36 53 E3
Watermore Clo. BS36 53 F2
Watleys End Rd. BS36 53 A2
Watters La. BS36 53 F3
Wayside Clo. BS36 53 E3
West Ridge. BS36 53 E2
Western Av. BS36 53 C1
Willow Way. BS36 53 F3
Winchcombe Rd. BS36 53 D1
Woodend Rd. BS36 53 E3
York Gdns. BS36 53 C2

WOTTON- UNDER-EDGE

Adeys La. GL12 52 B5
Bear St. GL12 52 B5
Bearlands. GL12 52 B6
Beechwood Gro. GL12 52 D4
Blackquarries Hill.
  GL12 52 D4
Bradley Rd. GL12 52 A4
Bradley St. GL12 52 C5
Brickfields. GL12 52 B6
Browns Piece. GL12 52 B5
Cherry Orchard. GL12 52 C5
Chipping Clo. GL12 52 B5
Chipping Gdns. GL12 52 B5
Church St. GL12 52 C5
Church Walk. GL12 52 C5
Clarence Rd. GL12 52 B5
Coombe La. GL12 52 D4
Coombe Rd. GL12 52 C4
Cotswold Gdns. GL12 52 C5
Court Meadow. GL12 52 C5
Court Orchard. GL12 52 C5
Culverhay. GL12 52 B5
Dryleaze. GL12 52 A5
Dryleaze Ct. GL12 52 A5
Dryleaze Gdns. GL12 52 A5
Durns Rd. GL12 52 A5
Ellerncroft Rd. GL12 52 A4
Fountain Cres. GL12 52 C5
Gloucester Row. GL12 52 C5
Gloucester St. GL12 52 C5
Haw St. GL12 52 A5
Hentley Tor. GL12 52 C5
High St. GL12 52 B5
Hill Rd. GL12 52 C5
Holywell Rd. GL12 52 C5
Jays Mead. GL12 52 C5
Knapp Rd. GL12 52 C5
Lisle Pl. GL12 52 A4